Spongeman to President
45 Years of ups and downs with Boston United

By
John Blackwell

In collaboration with
George Wheatman

Published March 2019
by
Chris Cook Print
Boston
Lincolnshire
PE21 6SY

Telephone 01205 355355
sales@chriscookprint.co.uk
www.chriscookprint.co.uk

Foreword by John Matson

who retired from the BBC in 2018 after 50 years
as a football commentator and reporter

I must have been seven or eight years old when my uncle first took me to Boston United. Darwen Matson worked in the outfitters Cheers, and my uncle Stan was a funeral director with Carr's.

Although I was not born and bred a "yellowbelly", both sides of my parents' families came from Boston. My father William was a product of Swineshead, and served over 40 years in the Methodist ministry. My mother Gwendoline, who he married in 1940, came from the Harrison family who lived for many years in Sleaford Road close to Wyberton Chain Bridge. So even though I was born in Salford, and lived my early life in south-east London, most of my family holidays were spent with grandparents in Boston.

I remember the uncles coming down to London to join my father and I at White Hart Lane for the third round F.A. Cup tie in 1956, when Boston United put up a great fight at Tottenham, before losing to a team that included the likes of Danny Blanchflower.

So, my affection for Boston United was well established when I first met John Blackwell. In those days, and for many years afterwards, the club secretary was the central figure behind the scenes. But that does not do justice to the immense role John and his wife Maureen played in the life of Boston Unit ed.

They were in the Midland League then. The biggest game of the season was against nearby rivals Peterborough United, and it often fell on Boxing Day. It seems amazing now, but the crowd at Shodfriars Lane (the name of the ground before it became York Street) was somewhere around 10,000.

The club's fortunes swung many different ways in the 60 years that followed. I remember how excited I was when United finally achieved Football League status, and I remember going to watch them play at Gigg Lane against Bury - a match which completed my "92 Club" membership as it was the last football league ground I visited.

My family's interest did not end there. When my son Fred was a very young lad, I took him down   to the ground to meet John and he came away with both home and away shirts which he proudly wore for some years.

Of course, it was John who organised that, along with any number of functions and associated events that enabled United to survive all sorts of ups and downs.

Owners, chairmen, managers (notably Howard Wilkinson and Jim Smith) and players came and went, but the Blackwells were always there, devoting many hours to the task of keeping the club going.

I often thought John could have moved to a bigger club - I am sure he had many offers - but he had Boston United carved on him somewhere!!! Nobody I met in football - not even in the rarified environment of the Premier League - gave so much time and effort into theclub.

John has at last put his experiences into print, and not before time. I am sure this book will bring back many happy memories and serve as a permanent reminder of how much the club owes to a man who will always be regarded as "Mr Boston United".

John Motson
December 2018

Introduction

All good things must come to an end, or so they say. But I never planned for my time with Boston United to come to an end. I had enjoyed it so much. A job that, for so many years, I had loved, despite the trials and tribulations; despite the long hours and not particularly good pay; despite the worries and, sometimes, heartache. Football, and particularly, Boston United was my life.

In hindsight, of course, I should have planned for the future, for retirement but, while many people live for the day when they no longer have to go to work, I thought it had no end. When the day came to leave York Street, I was like a little boy lost, and did not know what to do with myself. Nowhere to go, nothing to do. It is better now, of course. Time has a way of enforcing changes and, with the help of friends and family, my routine has changed - but I would still rather be working.

Luckily, I was made President of the club. A title with no purpose, some would say, but it has enabled me to travel to matches and keep in touch with the many friends and contacts I have made over the years.

Realistically, I knew that with changes on the horizon, and especially with plans for a new ground, my type of old-fashioned football administrator was becoming a dinosaur in the present day. After all, who would want someone who made arrangements by telephone, letter or personal contact, at a time when computers were taking over the world? I was not computer literate, and had no ambition to be and, keen not to stand in the way of the club's progress, I opted for retirement, despite not quite knowing what that had in store for me.

Write a book, I had been urged. I had kept many scrapbooks, and cuttings, and had so many memories, but how would that translate into a book?

George Wheatman, Sports Editor of the Boston Standard during my days in Boston League football with Real Towell, and at the time when I joined United, and subsequently Editor of the Standard and founder-Editor of the Target Series of Newspapers, was one person who had encouraged me to record my memories in print, and has now helped me do this.

It has helped fill the gaping hole in my life, re-kindled the long-standing friendship with George, and we have both enjoyed the hours of reminiscing. I hope that you will also enjoy our efforts to put on permanent record vital years of Boston United's history, the controversy and success, and I hope that you, too, will revel in the nostalgia which embraces not only football but, along the way, some of the town's social history.

John Blackwell

4

In the beginning

The year 1947 is recorded as one of the coldest ever in this country. I avoided that particularly bleak February by a few months - seven in fact - and was born in a much warmer September of that year. My father Maurice and mother Irene Ellen added to the post-war baby boom by just one. I was an only child, born at my grandmother's home next to the police house in King Street, Kirton. I was christened John, but some of my oldest friends, mainly from schooldays, call me Henry. I was given that name by schoolmate, Graham Marshall. I never fathomed why.

Father Maurice and mother Irene Ellen holding a very young John Blackwell

My love for sport in general, and football in particular, was probably in my genes because my dad was a much respected local goal-scoring centre forward with Kirton Town and Sutterton. When he joined the Royal Air Force, and while serving at Manby, he had a trial with Burnley and, ironically, there was a Boston United connection with that game. Playing in the same team was the former United goalkeeper of early post-war years, Jock Bayne. Subsequently I had many chats with Jock who lived out his old age in Boston, dying, I believe, at the age of 90-plus.

Just as the weather was mellow in September 1947, I was surrounded by warmth, love and encouragement from my parents, sadly no longer with us. Dad died on August 17th 1990, and mum also died in the month of August, 18 years later on the 25th.

John at the age of 3

At the time of my birth, dad was a carpenter-joiner with Langleys, in Kirton, and was always a much admired tradesman. Mum was a housekeeper and nanny at Graves Farm, Frampton, and one of the children she looked after was Bob Graves, whose ability as a goalkeeper took him into Lincoln City's first team before he quit the game and turned to rugby.

While I was young, we moved to 78 Freiston Road in Boston, nextto Waples the tinsmiths who will be remembered by many older Bostonians. More important for me was the fact that we were also near Burgess's Pit playing field, a hive of football activity for boys of all ages and abilities.

The start of my involvement with football, winner of a fancy dress competition at primary school

That was where I honed my own soccer skills alongside some of the town's best footballing products, some of whom moved into the professional game. Players who graced the Burgess Pit "academy" included the likes of Gordon Bolland, who went on to star on famous grounds around the country with Chelsea, Millwall and Norwich City, and who ended his playing days by bringing his elegant style back to Boston with the United. Alan Ashberry, who went to Arsenal and also later returned to play for the United, and Mick Robinson (Chelsea and Peterborough), and lots of other good local players, were among the talent to emerge from the "Pit". Football-crazy youngsters spent every minute they could playing there.

I was lucky to attend Tower Road Primary School, not far from home and near to the all-important Burgess Pit playing field, because sport was high on the agenda there. Somebody must have thought that I had some ability as a footballer because I was called up to play for the school team a

**John aged 7 at
Tower Road Primary School**

6

year before the usually accepted age, and in my last year there I was captain of the team which won the Woodthorpe Cup competed for by the Primary Schools in the area.

I played in goal at that time, despite my lack of inches. All those of you who know me will have noted that any subsequent growth has not been upwards and that, perhaps, was the reason that I eventually moved to play centre forward .

Anyway, for the time being, I was stuck with the goalkeeping role, and enjoying it enormously, and continued to do so when moving to Kitwood Boys School where I came under the influence of super-enthusiastic sports teachers Wilf Robinson and David Laver. Many other boys will have enjoyed their help and encouragement.

Sport was my main subject at Kitwood and I was a member of the Under 13s team which had 13 fixtures, won them all, scoring 116 goals in the process, many of those being netted by John Wilson, Dennis Reeson and Brian Thirkell, The defence was pretty handy too as we conceded only three times. Perhaps the goalkeeper played a part in that!

John Wilson has been a regular supporter of United over the years, Dennis was highly rated as he moved into senior football and starred for Boston FC (now Boston Town), among other teams at semi-professional level, and Brian, nicknamed Socket, went on to be a prolific scorer in Boston League football.

An omen for the future? We played in the black and amber colours of Boston United, only in hoops.

I was goalkeeper and captain, and also played for the under 14s and under 1Ss (while still eligible for the Under 13s) and was selected for the Holland Schools Under 1Ss representative side although two years younger than many boys in the team.

One of my many newspaper cuttings, yellowing and faded, reminds me that one Holland Boys team of that era was: Blackwell and Cebula (Kitwood Boys School), Wiseman (Peele School, Long Sutton), Oglesbee and Holley (KBS), Elleray (Boston Grammar School}, Walmsley (Kirton}, Bradshaw and Dann (KBS}, Hobart and Cater (BGS).

I continued to represent Holland Schools up to leaving school at the age of 16, and also had a trial for England Schools, where maybe my lack of height went against me because I did not progress from the trials. While tasting representative football, however, I did sample what it was like playing on United's York Street ground, and also Grimsby Town's Blundell Park.

The late Terry Thorne, who went on to play for Ipswich Town, Notts County, Boston United and Boston FC, was the captain of Holland Boys, and this was the team that lost 4-1 to Grimsby Boys: Blackwell (KBS), Willerton (Gleed School, Spalding), Morley (BGS), Stevens (Kirton), Deaton (Gleed), Thorne (BGS), Collishaw (BGS), Foster (KBS), Harvey (Kirton), French (Gleed) and Day (BGS).

A match report in one of my old scrapbooks suggests that the defeat would have been heavier had it not been for some fine saves by goalkeeper Blackwell!

Kitwood Boys won the Pitcher Cup twice, beating Peele School, Long Sutton, in one final and Sleaford Secondary Modern School in the other. I played in goal in one, and centre forward in the other.

A cutting from an old scrapbook reported that Blackwell played in goal and at centre forward in our 3-0 win over Sleaford but, however versatile I may have thought I was as a 15-year-old, that versatility did not allow for saving goals and scoring them in the same match.

The bit I did like from that report was, hopefully, more accurate and read as follows: "Blackwell, who chased every ball anywhere near the Sleaford goal, gained his reward when he beat a defender, and swivelled round to shoot past the helpless 'keeper.

"The centre forward later broke through, drew the goalkeeper out of position, and rolled the ball across the goalmouth to present Dann with a gift goal."

It was his second of the match and the Kitwood team was: David Johnson, Michael Goodson, Jim Dransfield, Ian Kirkham, Peter Holley, Alan Cebula, Fred Barnard, Robert Dann, John Blackwell, Les Bradshaw and Ian Stewart.

At one stage in all this footballing frenzy, Dennis Reeson and I went for a trial at Peterborough United. Both of us thought that we had done all right but we heard nothing from the club. The next day, however, the manager - Derek Dougan - was sacked

Football was not the onlysportthat I enjoyed.

I also represented my school at athletics, cricket, cross country and even gymnastics. Oh where did all that energy go? Sapped by the passing years, and the long hours and stress working for Boston United, no doubt!

I won the Holland Schools Cross Country Championship at Spalding's Gleed School, and went on to represent the District in the English Schools Cross Country

8

Championship.

In my final year at Kitwood Boys School, I won every event I entered on sports day, and again represented Holland Schools. I was made a School Prefect in my final year, and I can honestly say that I thoroughly enjoyed my time at the school. Sport played a major role in that enjoyment.

While I was enjoying my carefree, sports-laden, school days, my dad was working hard to establish his own business, after leaving Hookers Builders, in Boston's High Street, another name from the town's past.

Perhaps he harboured the thought that his only son might succeed him in the carpentry, joinery and decorating business. I don't know, but I did work for him on leaving school, although football occupied more of my thoughts than the day job. Tottenham Hotspurs was my favourite team.

From an early age, probably five or six years old, dad had taken me to the Shodfriars Lane ground to watch Boston United.

We would sit in the old wooden stand, now replaced, and there were big crowds in those days when United competed with a good side in the old, competitive, Midland League.

I have a vague recollection of the first-ever floodlit match at Shodfriars Lane, against Corby Town, which attracted a reported attendance of 11,000. There was also the visit of a Ugandan touring side which stands out because their team played in bare feet.

I became a regular visitor to "Shoddys", if not with my dad, then with friends, often cycling to the ground.

Long-time United supporters will recall that the dressing rooms were at the far end, now site of the Starlight Rooms. Fred Tunstall was groundsman. Many would argue that he was the best player ever to sign for Boston United, having played at the highest level for England and Sheffield United pre-war.

He was manager at Boston before taking on the role of groundsman. I remember he "painted" the markings on the pitch with a paint brush - again a far cry from today.

Another of United's long line of outstanding goalkeepers, England B international Ray King, was manager during my early visits to the ground. In his biography, Hands, Feet and Balls he wrote little of his time at Boston, only this: "After three

9

successful seasons at Boston, the club decided to reinstate Ray Middleton, a former manager of the club. The chairman who had engaged my own services, Mr (Horace) Luesby, eventually resigned after I had been there a couple of years, and a former chairman of the club, a millionaire called Malkinson, took over again. Unfortunately for me he was intent on having Middleton back. Apparently they were great friends."

Getting to a United match back in those days was, to a boy like me, an adventure in itself. The town was buzzing on match days with an influx of supporters from the surrounding villages, many arriving by bus, and, with the plans to split Boston in two with the building of John Adams Way still many years off, you had to squeeze down Shodfriars Lane. I say squeeze because it was often a tight fit on a busy Saturday, or for a floodlit night match which always seemed so special.

You entered The Lane near Shodfriars Hall, still a landmark building in the town, and shuffled your way down towards the old Gliderdrome skating rink before turning left into the turnstile.

I remember that there was a big news story when a fire destroyed the skating rink and, on the Sunday morning me and some of my friends went to see the devastation caused by the blaze.

On match days a local character, Bertie Wilson, would amuse the crowd by running round the perimeter of the pitch at half-time, usually in his rolled down wellingtons. His drinking habits made him a regular visitor to the local court. Another man, Bob Smith, would don fancy dress for home games.

The Blackwell family eventually moved house from 78 Freiston Road to 24 Spilsby Road so that my father could use Dunmore's Garage as his business premises, but what a day he chose to move! It couldn't have been worse for me because I had to miss that momentous occasion when Boston United travelled to Derby County and thrashed the Rams 6-1 in the most famous of all their FA Cup wins. Of course a number of the Boston players, six I think, including goalkeeper player-manager Ray Middleton, had been released by Derby at various points in their soccer careers and, no doubt, they felt they had a point to prove. What a way to do it. I believe that this still stands as the biggest win in the FA Cup by a non-League club away to Football League rivals. Moreover, it was Derby's first home defeat of the season and they went on to win the Division Three championship that year.

United supporters of the 'fifties era will have that team etched in their memories: Ray Middleton, Ralph Robinson, Geoff Snade, Don Hazledine, Dave Miller, Tommy Lowder, Reg Harrison, Geoff Hazledine, Ray Wilkins, Johnny Birkbeck and Reg Howlett.

Dad made amends by taking me to see the next round when United earned rave reports in the national Press despite losing 4-0 on a heavy ground away to the star-studded Tottenham Hotspur, a bittersweet result because Spurs were my favourite League club. On arrival home from that match we found Boston heavily covered in snow.

When I left school I worked alongside Dad and his trusted right hand man, Ron Brewster, another highly respected tradesman, but football was never far from my thoughts.

I played locally in the Boston and District League and the Youth League for Boston Athletic, Boston United Reserves and the Lincolnshire Standard, before joining the newly-formed Towell FC who competed in the equally new Boston Sunday League.

We played at Rosebery Avenue, on the council-owned pitches, on the uneven Mountain's Field at the top of Rosebery Avenue and now a built-up area, and pitch-shared with Lin-Can FC at Long Hedges.

Towell FC was formed by Geoff Rivett, Joe Sykes and Derek Paine at Towells Woodyard which was situated at Bargate End and is now a car park adjoining Bargate Drain and Bargate Bridge.

TOWELL F.C. Back Row - Left to Right: Steve Rogers, Alan Hooker, Bernie Brothwell, Ron Butler, Malcolm Bell, David Ogden, Alan Elkington. Front Row - Left to Right: Mick Stevens, Dennis Reeson, John Blackwell, Male Stares and Graeme Brown.

Little was it realised at the outset what an impact this team was to have on local football but, playing in all-red kit, we were so successful that it was decided to form a Saturday side as well and, with headquarters at Cyril Burton's pub, the King's Head, in Emery Lane, we wrote to the world-famous Spanish club, Real Madrid, seeking permission to use their name, and played in their colours of all-white. Cyril became our chairman.

We received their blessing, and permission to use their badge which they sent along with other souvenirs, and entered the lower end of the Boston League. Progress was rapid and we soon worked our way into the top division and fielded the best Saturday and Sunday teams in the area, the Saturday team winning the Boston League championship three times, in seasons 1965-66, 1967-68 and 1968-69. I was lucky enough to play for both Saturday and Sunday teams.

Eventually we felt that we needed our own ground and, with the kind co-operation and permission of farmer Mr Tunnard, we moved to Tunnard's Park, Boston West.

Towells became the magnet for many of the best players in the district, and we had reserve and youth teams also playing at Tunnard's Park. I accepted the invitation to become secretary, my first step into football administration.

REAL TOWELL F.C. Back Row - Left to Right: Ron Franklyn (Physio), John Blackwell (Secretary/ Player), Norman Mottram, Alan Hooker, Ken Bonner, Malcolm Bell, Peter Bird, Mick Bastow, Steve Rogers, David Coulson, Front Row - Left to Right: Barry Bunce, Tony Winn, Male Stares, Dennis Reeson and Tony Scrupps . Mascot: Bernard Barty

12

First of all we used two old caravans as changing rooms, but our ambition outgrew these and we purchased two chalets from Derbyshire Miners Welfare Centre, in Roman Bank, Skegness.

A team spirit second to none had developed in the club, and this was in evidence as we descended in force on Skegness one weekend to dismantle the chalets and erect them back in Boston as our new dressing rooms.

The togetherness was something to behold. Players were the best of mates and socialised together, and this was reflected in the results on the field as we became a force to be reckoned with throughout the county.

Highlight for the Saturday side was when we won the Lincolnshire Junior Cup, beating Grimsby Borough Police 4-2 in the final on Boston United's ground before a crowd of 1200.

The Grimsby Police team was formidable opposition in the competition almost every year, including in their side a number of ex-professionals, who had joined the Force. Many had Scottish accents.

Unfortunately , I missed out on playing in the final, although I played in the semi-final. Regular goalkeeper, Ken Bonner, had recovered from injury in time to play in the big match, and I could not even be on the subs bench because no substitutes were allowed in those days.

The Towell team on that memorable day was: Ken Bonner, David Coulson, David Ogden, Dennis Reeson, Malcolm Bell, Peter Bird, Barry Bunce, Tony Winn, Alan Hooker, Norman Mottram and Male Stares.

Real Towell became the first Boston League side to win the Lines Junior Cup after the successes of the formidable Bicker Rangers team, and they gradually ousted the village team as the top club in the area.

It was always satisfying to be part of a rare victory against Bicker, and, on one occasion, I had the satisfaction of scoring the winning goal against them for Boston United Reserves in the Fishtoft Cup final.

We reckoned Real Towell was one of the best, if not THE best, local team in the county, beating pretty well every side put before us, and we were always up for a challenge.

That came when we spotted an article in the national Press about a team from the Grantham area, run by a man from Belvoir Castle, claiming that they must be

13

European champions because they had won a tournament on the Continent. They were looking for challengers and we answered their call to play at Woolsthorpe.

Well, their win in Europe must have been against pretty weak opposition because we beat them 35-0, Male Stares and myself each scoring double figures.

Not only that, we wiped the slate with them at darts and skittles at a pub in Redmile, where they were based, in the evening. Nevertheless, we established a friendship and visited them for a night out on many other occasions.

Two of the most important decisions of my life were made while I was with the Towell teams. Now, I have heard it said that nothing good comes from hanging about on street corners. Well, I would challenge that.

With the Towell headquarters based at the King's Head, in Emery Lane, we used to meet there before matches, at weekends and most evenings. Sometimes, however, we had to wait for the pub to open and a group would congregate at the foot of Town Bridge, chatting, watching the world go by and, of course, as young men were designed to do, commenting on the girls passing by.

One young lady caught my eye as she walked past with her pet poodle on several occasions. I knew also that she worked as receptionist at the nearby White Hart Hotel. I had seen her when we went in there for drink, and the attraction grew. Eventually, I plucked up the courage to ask her for a date. Luckily for me, she agreed.

The young lady was Maureen Forman, who lived with her parents at the Axe and Cleaver public house in West Street. The relationship flourished and we were married at Boston's Holy Trinity Church on October 11th 1973.

John Platt, a talented local footballer of that time, was my best man. Maureen's bridesmaids were her sister Jackie, and friend Susan Mitcham. I was 26; Maureen was 23.

At the time of our marriage she was a clerk at Norprint, the label manufacturers who were probably the biggest employers in Boston.

She was well aware of my passi on for football, and even agreed that our wedding arrangements could be built around the demands of my new job with Boston United . She must have been smitten!

We exchanged our vows on a Thursday because United had a match two days later. The reception was at the Richmond Rooms at the Gliderdrome, and our honeymoon in the Spanish resort of Lloret de Mar started on the Monday and finished on the Thursday because, yes, you have guessed it, United had a match on the Satu rday. We started married life in a flat above Vamplews the builders, in Main Ridge- number 69.

Since then we have been blessed with two daughters, Lisa Dawn and Katie Louise, and Maureen has been the rock in my life, and has supported me during all those years with Boston United , whatever the job has thrown at us and, believe me, there have been a lot of difficult times, as well as good days. Wife of the general manager at Boston United - and, I guess, at many football clubs - cannot expect a husband who works regular hour s. More likely seven days a week, and long days at that.

Lisa was born on May 3rd 1978, and Katie on February 19th 1982.

John and Maureen on their wedding day October 11th 1973 at Holy Trinity Church, Boston

The day after Lisa arrived in this world, I was at Manchester City's Maine Road Ground where Boston United were playing Matlock Town, inspired at that time by the Fenoughty brothers, in the final of the Northern Premier League Cup . We lost , but it was still very late when we left Manchester, and I did not arrive back in Boston until 5am . Just as I entered the house, the 'phone rang. It was Pilgrim Hospital. Our new baby was very poorly. She had been born with a heart defect.

It was pouring with rain as I cycled to the hospital to hear the news that Lisa would have to be moved to the Northern General Hospital at Winkobank, Sh effield . She was so poorly that she was baptised while she was there.

Maureen had had a difficult time at the birth and was not well enough to travel with her, but a couple of days later we were able to travel to

Attending a wedding... It's amazing how fashion goes around in circles!

Sheffield where she was transferred to the children's hospital.

However, Lisa was still very poorly and they decided that they could not carry out the essential operation at Sheffield. We had the choice of moving her to Southampton, Liverpool or London's famous Great Ormond Street hospital.

We chose the latter and Lisa had an operation called the "shunt" to help her before another major operation in 1991. This time was even more scary for Maureen and I as there were severe complications and , at one stage, Lisa was given only hours to live. She had four more operations in a 24-hour spell, and eventually came home on June 19th after a five-week stay in hospital.

That, however, was not the end of the trauma, and Lisa had to have major open heart surgery on December 19th 2005 at the Queen Elizabeth Hospital in Bir mingham . We spent Christmas Day at the hospital and ate our Christmas dinner off paper plates at the hospital cafe, that is Maureen and I, Katie and my mother, and Lisa's partner, David Whalley.

Having started married life in the Main Ridge flat, we moved to my parents old house at 24 Spilsby Road, Boston, after they built a new one at 17 Spilsby Road. Subsequently we lived in Princess Anne Road, had a spell in a temporary home in Spain Place in a cottage belonging to the Gliderdrome complex after we had sold the Princess Anne Road property, before moving to Buckingham Close where we have lived since 1999.

The second of those important decisions I mentioned earlier involved leaving the successful Towell soccer set-up to join Boston United in an administrative capacity. United had a new player-manager in Jim Smith, as part of chairman Ernest Malkinson's drive to re-establish the club as one of the top non-League teams in the country, and even strive for Football League status.

After the club had a season out of senior football, Don Donovan was recruited to mastermind the rise through the United Counties League and the West Midlands League into the new Northern Premier League . He had done this successfully, but it was felt that his job was completed with a mid-table position in the first NPL season .

So Jim was at the start of a new era. He had been released by Lincoln City and there were plenty of clubs wanting to sign the industrious midfielder, but Mr Malkinson was a persuasive man when he had a signing in mind . He had watched Jim play several times for Lincoln and thought he would make the ideal player-manager for United. The approach came, I would think, at a time when family man Jim was thinking about life after his playing career ended, so coming to Boston would be

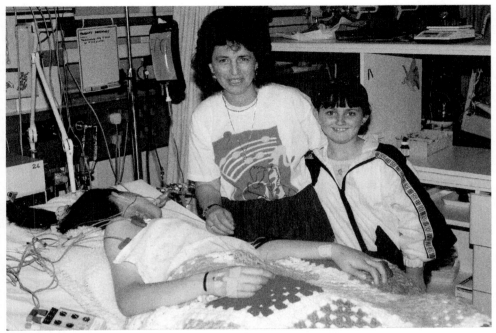

Maureen and Katie visiting Lisa after open heart surgery

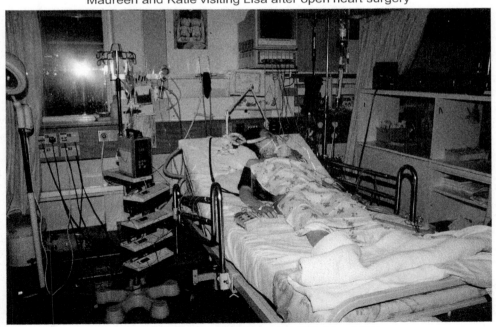

Great Ormond Street Hospital 17th May 1991

his first test as a manager .

He came to live in the town, moving from Doddington Road in Lincoln to Mayfair Gardens, just off Spilsby Road and, as I lived in Spilsby Road, our paths soon crossed. He discovered that I was involved in football, and we often chatted about the game in general.

So commenced a friendship that has lasted to this day, despite Jim's rise to the big time. But there was an early altercation . . . When he discovered that I was running the successful Towells Boston League set-up, he asked if United could use the Tunnards Park pitch for a private pre-season match against Louth United, as the York Street ground was not ready.

I agreed, but then did not hear a thing from him for weeks, until the day before the scheduled match in fact . Because I had heard nothing, we had not worked on the pitch, the grass was long, and we had the regular problem with molehills. There was no way we could now get the ground ready, and I told him that it was no longer available.

Jim was not pleased, to say the least. He had to postpone the fixture at short notice and blamed me for all the problems caused. Strangely, after the initial blow up, we became firm friends, and Jim proved that he did not carry grudge s.

After a while he invited me to leave Towells and join Boston United to help look after the reserves and youth teams because I knew the local soccer scene, and players, so well. It was not an easy decision after all the success and camaraderie we had enjoyed at Towells, but I could not resist the temptation to move up to semi-professional football.

Jim was doing pretty well everything at York Street, and needed some help. He signed the players, prepared the pitch, organised the training, helped with commercial activities and even gave a hand to re-decorate the boardroom. Years later his proud boast was that some of the wallpaper he put up was still there.

Dad was as helpful and flexible as ever and allowed me to continue working for him while dipping my toe into life at Boston United. It was a great opportunity to move into senior non-League football in my spare time.

Sadly- and I don't want to infer that they could not live without me - this appeared to be the start of the decline of Towe lls. The father of one of the players, Mr Dungworth, took over from me as secretary, but, within a couple of years they had folded.

Maureen and I became good friends of the Smiths, Jim, his wife Yvonne, and their three daughters, and we often met up socially, and also baby sat the children.

I helped in many ways at the club and went to training with the first team at Balderton Sports Centre, Newark. It was interesting mixing with players who were formerly full-time professionals now stepping into the part-time game.

I also helped with the reserves and youth team, alongside John Hall, and began to take the first steps which eventually led me into full-time administration with the club.

Peter Jackson was first team trainer, former manager and ex-England B international goalkeeper, Ray Middleton, was secretary and organiser of the bingo ticket fundraising scheme which was one of the biggest in the country.

Ernest and Sydney Malkinson were at the helm, directors were Alf Bell, Les Bray and Jim Lees, and Ernest's son Pat was on hand to help anywhere required.

Those were the days when the Gliderdrome was the hub of entertainment in Boston, attracting the biggest names in the music business to packed Saturday gigs, while bursting at the seams on bingo nights. It was a mecca for pop fans from all over the country, reputed to be the largest dance hall in the UK and, even today, is remembered with affection by many music idols who visited the Glider at the start of their careers.

The football club had an office in Shodfriars Hall before moving to combined cottages in front of the Gliderdrome, 7 and 9 Spain Place, where Ray Middleton was helped by his wife Murial to organise the bingo fundraiser.

I was still working with my father when received a call from Jim Smith and Ernest Malkinson with the news that Ray Middleton had been taken ill and was in hospital. They wanted someone, with some experience, to take over secretarial duties while he was off work, and urged me to ask my father if I could go to the club full-time for as long as was required.

Dad knew only too well how keen I was to join the football club and, as ever, agreed for

Ray Middleton

19

me to go until Ray recovered.

As well as doing the secretarial work, I also helped on the fundraiser, a small bingo ticket which, I believe, cost 5p at the time. Tickets were sold all over Lincolnshire, Norfolk, Cambridgeshire, Nottinghamshire and Derbyshire, raising money to help the new manager re-shape the team.

Key players were retained from Don Donovan's squad, and Jim added to these by signing a number of ex-League players. As well as competing in the Northern Premier League , United were also in the Eastern Professional Floodlight League and the Lincolnshire League .

Although helping out with some first team duties, I was still involved with the reserves and youth team, as well as being secretary. Then I received a call one Friday from Jim. Could I go and help collect the club's van, and some equipment from Peter Jackson's house? Later that day I was asked to be trainer for the first team the following day for the home match against Ellesmere Port, as Pete was no longer available . I remember that match well. It ended in a 0-0 draw and was another major step in my life with Boston United.

We played the same team again the following week, away in the FA Cup. We travelled on Friday afternoon to a hotel in the Wirral. It was a terrible journey in wet, snowy conditions, and we woke up the next morning to find deep snow everyw here. The match was obviously in doubt, and when we arrived at the ground the pitch was covered in snow to a depth of three inches. Nevertheless, referee Les Hayes, of Doncaster, decided that it was playable.

I remember that it was so cold that we had to park the team coach next to the ground's boundary wall so that the only travelling director, Ernest Malkinson, could watch the match from the comparative warmth of the 'bus. Conditions were farcical, but we played really well and, on the coldest day I can remember in my career in football, United won 3-0. After the match, Mr Malkinson gave me the task of searching out bottles of whisky to purchase for the players to warm them up.

I remember that Howard Wilkinson, Bobby Svare and Robbie Coates scored the Boston goal s. Despite the awful weather, a coach load of hardy supporters made the long trip to cheer on the team. Ellesmere Port had a big, physical team, and one of their players, Gerry Casey, was sent off in the first half . Another formidable player in their side was Leo Skeete, a big, muscular centre forward who, a few years later, played for Mossley against United in an FA Trophy semi-final tie.

Thinking of those early days at the club brings back many memorie s. It was all new, and exciting, to me, and I had a close-up view of matches as trainer.

I remember a match at Chorley (the ground still looks the same all these years later) on another atrocious day, heavy rain and flooded pitch, when United left back Mick Hopkinson (ex-Derby County) sustained a badly broken leg. After a long hold-up, he was taken to Preston Hospital. We followed up after the match to see if he would be coming home with us. It was, however, such a bad break that Mick had to stay in hospital for almost a week, and I don't think he ever played again.

The manager took us to an Indian restaurant near the hospital before we set off for home at about midnight.

There are still vivid memories of the long hours spent on tiring coach journeys. When we played in the Eastern Premier Floodlit League we visited lots of clubs down south at a time when there were no motorways in that part of the country where we played the likes of Romford, Chelmsford City, Dartford, Cambridge City and United, and we had to leave Boston at lunch time to travel down the A1 to London and then make our way out of London to these grounds, often arriving home at 3-4am.

There were also long, exhausting journeys to Northern Premier League grounds such as Wigan Athletic (the old Springfield Park ground}, Bangor City in North Wales (a huge journey), Ashington in the North East, Scarborough and Macclesfield, often in midweek, again with no help from motorways which were still a thing of the future. There were no M62, M1, M6 motorways to cut the travelling time. It was all minor roads and traffic jams and long overnight journeys.

Eventually Ray Middleton decided that he was fit enough to return to work part-time, which would still leave me part-time work at the club while also going back to work part-time with my dad. Ray came to watch the home match against Lancaster City on Easter Monday, and decided to come into work the next day.

After a morning back at the office, he drove to his Willoughby Road home for lunch but, sadly, was found in a collapsed state in his car on the bungalow drive, and died later that day. This was in 1978. This was a sad time for his devoted wife, for his friend Ernest Malkinson, and all at the football club as Ray had been a key figure in some of the best times Boston United had ever experienced.

As always, however, life had to go on, and his death finally presented the chance for me to establish myself at United. Little did I realise that a small market town football club could, over the forthcoming years, provide so much drama, controversy, heartache, friendship, excitement, disappointment, tears of joy and sadness, and fulfilment.

In the following pages I will attempt to tell you all about it from my point of view and hope that my journey down Memory Lane will also stimulate your memories and set you thinking about teams, players and matches from the past.

Much of that journey was travelled alongside members of the Malkinson family, three generations in fact, and it might be appropriate at this point to emphasise that many of the best moments enjoyed by Boston United have been thanks to their commitment, investment and enthusiasm.

Few football club chairmen, would suggest, have loved the game of football more than Mr Ernest Malkinson and few have had a better knowledge of the game or had a better understanding of footballers and their idiosyncrasies.

Jim Smith, who went on to have experience of a variety of football club chairmen, rated Mr Malkinson as one ofthe best he ever worked with and, in his

Ernest Malkinson

biography, "It's only a game", paid a warm tribute to the man who gave him his first opportunity in management.

A later manager Albert Phelan was, on one occasion, incensed at the attitude of a section of the crowd towards Mr Malkinson after a disappointing display in a pre-season county cup match. In fact, he took these critics to task in the Boston Standard with an uncharacteristic straight-talking comment.

"However anyone can stoop to criticising Mr Malkinson after what he has done for the town and club is beyond me," he told the Standard. "The senseless ones among the supporters think we have money to burn. They forget that if Mr Malkinson had not sunk money into the club over the years, it may not be in existence now".

Feared for my job

A number of businessmen moved in and out of the boardroom as directors of the club during my time with United, but in the early years I was working for members of the Malkinson family whose investment in the club, through time and money, was immense. Pat Malkinson, after his term as chairman, later revealed that they had "supported the club financially to the tune of hundreds of thousands of pounds over the years."

The main men were brothers Ernest and Sydney, and they were as different as chalk and cheese. Mr Ernest was the real football fanatic and, with a large cigar his constant companion, was the father figure around the club. The only other sport that tempted him away from football was showjumping, and that was because his daughter Claire was an accomplished rider and a constant source of pride for him. He lavished a lot of money on horses and all the accessories that go with showjumping - a far cry from the days when he was involved in the more working class sport of pigeon racing. He and wife Frances lived on Wainfleet Road in Boston.

Mr Sydney, who lived with wife Gladys in Spilsby Road before moving to Ferndale Drive, was a different kind of character, quiet, careful and thoughtful about everything he did. He drove an old Hillman car for many years, whereas Ernest had a number of smart cars.

Mr Ernest was well-known, and highly visible, in football circles; Mr Sydney less so, but an important figure at the club nevertheless. Together, they were a formidable, shrewd business partnership with an eye for the opportunity, something they showed by turning their Gliderdrome into one of the top music venues in the country in the heyday of touring groups, and then packing the Glider with followers of bingo when this became a big craze .

Most of the top groups performed at the Gliderdrome, but I remember the ultra cautious Mr Sydney once telling me that he could have booked the one and only Beatles, but he thought their fee of £45 was too much!

Other directors in my early days included Wrangle farmer, Les Bray, Sydney Burgess, a director of cattle dealers and exporters, Frans Buitelaar, former referee Jim Lees, who worked for the Royal Insurance Company, and was local representative on the Lincolnshire Football Association, Alf Bell, who became catering manager at the Gliderdrome after owning the popular Cherry Corner snack bar at the junction of the Market Place with Strait Bargate in Boston, and George Jackson, who worked at the Gliderdrome and was elected vice-chairman.

Mr Ernest's son Pat, a constant companion and support to his father, joined the board shortly before we went to Wembley in the FA Trophy final, and was chairman when we played that epic match. By that time advancing years were taking their toll on Mr Ernest and he was in poor health. Nevertheless, he had the courage and determination to attend the final which must have been one of his long-held dreams.

When he died in April 1986, at the age of 87, there were many people from the world of football at his funeral service in Boston Stump, including ex-United managers and players. He had been honoured by the Lincolnshire Football Association and the Northern Premier League for his service to football.

Pat Malkinson

In his biography Jim Smith revealed that Mrs Malkinson told him that Ernest closely followed the results of every team with which Jim was involved, and she said that his great wish was that he lived long enough to see him lead a team out at Wembley. In 1986 Jim led Queen's Park Rangers onto the hallowed turf in the final of the Milk Cup. Mr Malkinson died 20 minutes after the game had finished.

Jim wrote: "For me he was a founder member of the league of gentlemen - an absolute diamond. I could never thank him enough for what he did for me."

It was Sydney Burgess, during his stint as chairman, who promoted me from secretary to General Manager, adding extra responsibilities with the new title. Mr Burgess was chairman of Boston and District Football League for many years, and will also be remembered for producing the popular Scouts Gang Show which packed the old Regal cinema each year.

Over the years other businessmen to join the board included Stuart Bateman, from our sponsors Batemans Brewery, Leonard Shaw, a former Bostonian who owned property in the town but now living in Edgware, London, John Drewnicki, a Peterborough-based businessman who came when Peter Morris was appointed manager, Dick Carrington, a keen supporter and good friend of Pat Malkinson, Roy Hackford, another faithful supporter who worked at Johnsons Seeds, Brian James, who worked at the club's accountants, Mr Sydney's son, Stephen, who worked at the Gliderdrome, and another local businessman, Tim Ruck.

I enjoyed working with the Malkinsons who treated me and my family well, and embraced us as part of their wider family. Many of the best times Boston United, and their supporters, have enjoyed were built on their generosity. When they decided to distance themselves from the football club as their own business interests demanded more of their time and attention, things became more uncertain, less secure and I feared that the club was perilously close to collapse.

24

I am not ashamed to admit that I shed a few tears when, at lunchtime on Monday November 14th 2016, daughter Lisa broke the news to me that Pat Malkinson had died. He was 75 and had suffered a distressing battle against cancer.

The huge attendance at his funeral service in Boston Stump reflected the warmth with which he was regarded in the community, and far beyond. It was significant that there were people from all walks of life, rich and poor. His friendly smile captivated everyone.
He would have been so proud of the part his two grandsons played in the service.

Pat was not a director of Boston United when I first joined the club, but was very supportive of his father and was regularly present at the office and ground and, of course, the Gliderdrome, often accompanied by his dog Dougal.

Pat was a true gentleman who placed great importance on good manners, and showed great loyalty to friends and staff. Following the lead of his father and uncle, he became a special person in the history of Boston United, and was well respected in football circles. As was hinted at his funeral it was, perhaps, his support for others that caused him to suffer personal anguish, and great cost- not only monetary- in the worst chapter experienced by the club, and his family.

I worked alongside him at the club for about 25 years, he as chairman of directors while I was secretary-general manager. He was extremely supportive of United's work in the community and his non-judgemental friendship towards prisoners from North Sea Camp who worked at the ground was testament to the kind of man he was.

Pat was never afraid to get his hands dirty, whether it was erecting and dismantling the lottery stall we once had in Boston Market Place, digging drains on the York Street pitch or scaling a long, rickety ladder to replace a broken section at the top of the club flag pole- an operation that would have had today's Health and Safety officers aghast.

Pat was always very good to my family and, when I was asked to contact former players and managers to inform them of his death, invariably they remembered him with great affection, something which prompted many of them to travel to his funeral.

A lasting memory I will have of Pat's funeral will be of the dignity shown by his supportive and caring wife Pauline, and it is humbling to recall how she found the time, and courage, to talk to so many of the people who gathered at the Gliderdrome to reflect on Pat's life. I was touched when she came to talk to me on what must have been such a difficult day for her.

Trevor Killick, Chief Executive Dave Picket, Manager Neil Thompson, After Dinner Speaker Steve Kindon & Chairman Des Wood

It was towards the end of 2001 when Des Wood became involved as the new owner of Boston United. He was a Nottinghamshire business man with offices in Mansfield. I was never privy to his long-term plans but I believe his investment in the football club was to be the first step towards acquiring the ground and, no doubt, carrying out some kind of major development project. Alongside him was Trevor Killick, an accountant from Kirby in Ashfield. They came in at a time when United were poised to win the Conference (they clinched the title by victory at Hayes later that season after a nail-biting, fractious battle with Dagenham and Redbridge) and brought a very professional approach towards re-organising the administration at the club. They brought in Dave Picket as Chief Executive, a pleasant and excellent man with whom to work. He was a Bostonian, but lived in Grantham and had been involved in the building industry. He has remained on friendly terms with the club, often calling into the office to see how everyone was.

They took some of the pressure off me by making new appointment s. They brought in Birmingham-based Westpoint Media to take over commercial activities, and appointed Dick Carrington as stadium manager. The two ladies from Westpoint, Simone Steventon and Shelley Winwood, were a breath of fresh air and, ironically, they introduced Chestnut Homes as new shirt sponsors. Little did they know then the significance of that deal.

The Des Wood regime had to cope with the Football Association's investigation into contract irregularities which led to a ban being imposed on manager Steve Evans. For whatever reason, negotiations between Des Wood and the Malkinson family soured and finally collapsed so the football club was sold again.

I feared for my job when Jon Sotnick took over at United. He was a business man from the Cannock area of Staffordshire where he ran a recruitment agency. His partner in the acquisition of the club was Nigel Clempson, who had a building business with contracts in various parts of the country. Jon Sotnick rang me one Tuesday evening to inform me that he had acquired the football club, and that he would be coming over the next day to look around and speak to staff. Would I prepare a meeting room?

The Day of Destiny arrived and Chief Executive Dave Pickett was first in - and therefore the first to be told that his services were no longer required.

Neil Thompson, the popular manager of the day, and a true football man who had operated under great difficulties, was next to be sacked.

Then it was my turn. I fully expected to follow Dave and Neil out of the door but, surprise, surprise, I was told that my job was safe.

On reflection, I suppose that it was my experience and knowledge of how football is run administratively behind the scenes that made me useful to the newcomers. Football is not like any other business, and the Football Association and the various competitions have their own rules, regulations and rituals that have to be understood and followed - as some people within the club had already discovered.

Later that day, we were told that Steve Evans would be returning as manager - no surprise to the many fans who had predicted that Neil Thompson had been simply keeping the managerial seat warm until Mr Evans completed his period of suspension imposed by the FA. Coming back with Steve Evans was former player, the ultra fashion conscious Jim

Steve Evans

Rodwell, who always seemed to be vying to be the best dressed man in football. When he first played for United, in the reserves, he had a ponytail down to his waist.

I believe that this duo had been the movers behind Messrs Sotnick and Clempson acquiring United so it was no surprise to me that they were again quickly installed at the club. No surprise either was the appointment of Steve's brother Gee and his ever-loyal side-kick Paul Raynor to the coaching staff. Nigel Clempson's wife came in to do the books a few hours a week, and it was easy to work with her, a lovely lady.

Jon Sotnick was keen to move the club to a new stadium along the Boardsides, next to Boston Rugby Club, and plans were drawn up and I had to present the club's case to the Borough Planning Committee, but the idea was never given the go-ahead . I stressed to the councillors the importance of the football club to the town and district as a whole, and the reason that relocation was essential was that the York Street ground was getting old and not keeping pace with modern day stan dards. Indeed wou ld not do so without the expenditure of vast sums of money. I invited the committee to defer a decision on the application until they had visited the ground, and had seen its inadequacies for themselves. This visit never materialised.

David Newton, when addressing supporters after his take-over, suggested that the scheme did not get the support of planning officers and councillors because the financial information provided was not sufficiently detailed to establish the viability of the proposals. When he left Boston United, Jon Sotnick joined Football League club Darlington, and lived at Yarm . His first signing was Julian Joachim from The Pilgrims, the reported fee was £100, 000.

I know nothing of his whereabouts after he left Darlington, but his name cropped up when, in my new position as club President, I travelled with United to their match against Darlington 1883 at the start of the 2016 season. The game was played at Bishop Auckland and officials of the newly-formed Darlington club, were quick to seek me out, and the only person they wanted to talk about was Jon Sotnick. To say that he was not their favourite person would be an understatement. In a nutshell, they blamed him for the demise of the old Darlington team from the Football League into non-League football. Of course, I had no knowledge of what had gone on at Darlington, and could not comment on their views.

I found Nigel Clempson and his family to be very nice people and, a couple of years before my retirement, when United visited Hednesford Town, his company sponsored the match . He said that he was no longer associated with Mr Sotnick, and did not know where he was located.

Bailiffs were no strangers

There was a time when bailiffs did not need to ask directions to York Street. They had been there often enough to know the way off by heart, especially during the reign of Jon Sotnick and before the rescue by Chestnut Homes. There were, however, money problems long before this. I used to hate Fridays, pay day. Often there was not enough cash to meet the wage bill.

In the days when Sydney Burgess was chairman it was a ritual to go to his home in New Hammond Beck Road to seek his advice on how we were going to meet the wage bill. Usually he would have no idea, and made no offer of money himself. "I will leave it to you, John," he would say. There were a few people who helped out, but often it was the Malkinson family who came to the rescue.

On two occasions things became so desperate that I asked my mother-in-law, and my wife Maureen, if they could come up with the cash from their savings. Surprisingly, since they knew how precarious the financial situation was, they agreed, as long as I promised that they would get their money back. It took a long time to repay them, but eventually their loans were settled. That was an example of the tremendous support I have received from my family.

Bailiffs came in on almost a daily basis and I remember one day when they started loading all the trophies from the directors' room into their big white van. I pleaded with them not to do this, almost on my knees. They agreed, reluctantly, but only if I found the goods or money to settle the debt. I managed to do this, but I cannot remember how I did it. For 13 weeks, Craig Singleton, Maureen and myself worked without being paid a penny. It was a very difficult time for all of us, especially when we had to work at the ground, almost in the dark, as the front shutters were locked.

Around this time, Michael Chinn, owner of Staffsmart Ltd, was a regular visitor to the club and training, and was a key benefactor. I feared the demise of the club and pleaded with chief executive Jim Rodwell to let me call a public meeting in a last bid to save it. He was not keen on the idea but, after repeated pressure, agreed to let me go ahead.

Barry Pierrepoint agreed to help me. **An** experienced football administrator, and former chief executive at Leicester City and Portsmouth, and now a local councillor, he was at the club to carry out due diligence investigation on behalf of a Leeds business man who was said to be interested in taking over.

That crucial - and, as it turned out, life-saving meeting - was held on Father's Day 2007, at the York Street ground. In the car park, mingling with the 800 or so fans who showed their support by turning up, I met, and shook hands with, David

Newton, whose business, Chestnut Homes, was a key sponsor of the club . Little did I know at the time the significance of his presence. He said that he had come along just to give his support.

I addressed the supporters, somewhat emotionally, from the announcer's box in the York Street stand; Barry spoke from the pitch in front of the stand. We both stressed, again and again, that time was running out for the club. It was broke, and the future was grim, or rather non-existent, in our opinion. We pleaded for someone to come up with ideas to save the club, more importantly finance.

The encouraging thing was the number of people who attended the meeting; the discouraging thing was that nothing positive emerged from our appeal. Or so we thought . Shortly afterwards came the news that David Newton and Neil Kempster had stepped in to save the club. From that day to this, wages have been paid on time, and the reputation of the club, which had suffered enormously in the light of off-the-field activities, has gradually been restored.

I am sure that I can be excused for saying how proud I am for the part I played in securing the club's survival. I dread to think what could have happened had I not ignored the advice not to call that meeting.

Right from the outset of their takeover, Messrs Newton and Kempster did their best to run the club in a transparent manner and keep the fans info rmed. Quickly, they faced a meeting of supporters when David Newton did, in fact, confirm it was that public meeting which spurred him to act to save the club. I still have a copy of the uplifting, oh so welcome, speech he gave to the fans as reassurance that Barry and I had made the correct decision to appeal directly to the loyal followers of United.

The now-chairman recalled that Father's Day was "a lovely morning, and the pitch looked an absolute picture, and I must confess I have a real soft spot for this old ground." He continued: "I sat and contemplated what would happen if the deal did not go through with Standing Alone. The reality would be that the club would be wound up and this place, and Boston United Football Club, would be lost forever."

(*Standing Alone was the company which had been negotiating with Lavaflow, the then owners of Boston United and whose directors included Jonathan David Sotnick, James Richard Rodwell and John Gerard Evans. These negotiations appeared to have broken down when we called the public meeting. Standing Alone was named in the Company Voluntary Arrangement which is a legally binding agreement with creditors to allow a portion of debts to be paid back over a period of time).

David Newton revealed to the supporters that Jon Sotnick had invited Chestnut

Homes to become involved with a deal to re-locate the ground, but they had two issues with that:

1   They were involved in the club purely as sponsors.

2   The financial information provided was not sufficiently detailed to establish the viability of the proposals.

The chairman emphasised to the fans that he was not there for a land deal. He also stressed that his company entered into a situation that was "very complex", going on to explain: "It became clear that Standing Alone had entered into an option to acquire the shares of Lavaflow if, and when, a deal on the York Street ground could be concluded.

"As part of that deal, they had agreed to meet the day to day running costs of the club. This they failed to do, and were now proposing a new deal on different terms. "The new deal had been signed by the shareholders of Lavaflow but, despite a number of assurances, Standing Alone had failed to enter into the agreement. This not only left the club in limbo, the staff and players unpaid, but also put the CVA at risk."

Mr Newton continued to put his cards on the table in a manner which may have

Secretary John Blackwell, Chairman David Newton, Vice Chairman Neil Kempster & Commercial! Manager (now Secretary) Craig Singleton announcing the takover by Chestnut Homes

31

surprised su pporters. He ad ded: "I, like many fans, have been frustrated with shareholders of Lavaflow, and the way in which they appeared to be treating the club. However, now having looked at the history since Standing Alone came on the scene, I firmly believe that the proposed deal with Standing Alone was a good one for the club. It is the previous owners of Standing Alone who should take a long, hard look at themselves.

"They entered into a contract with Lavaflow, but did not honour their obligations, which has led to the near extinction of this football club.

"We believe that a football club is at the heart of a community, it is a large part of supporters' lives, and should be treated with respect. It is clear that they did not share that view."

He placed on record that Jim Rodwell, Phil Hanby and other Lavaflow shareholders had acted honourably towards Chestnut Homes.

Mr Newton revealed that in a meeting with Gerald Krasner (Mr Krasner is an insolvency expert who led a consortium of local businessmen in the takeover of Leeds United in 2004 and, as a partner in Bartfields, a recovery firm, was involved in assisting Bournemouth and Port Vale when they went into administration), and representatives of Standing Alone, Mr Krasner explained that "the point had been reached that either we concluded a deal to take over Standing Alone, and replace them in the CVA, or that the Inland Revenue were likely to insist that the club is wound up this week."

Phew. I knew things were bad, but I am not sure that I believed we were quite so close to falling off the precipice. Luckily the deal was done with Standing Alone, and terms were also agreed for the take over of Lavaflow.

Although Boston United had been given the kiss of life, there was a long recovery period ahead, but in David Newton and Neil Kempster, it had found two men who were determined not to allow a relapse in health.
They promised :

1   The club will be well run.

2   While we are here, everyone will be paid.

3   We will be prudent in the management of the club's fi nanc es.

4   We will strive for excellence on and off the pitch.

5   As finances permit, we will develop the youth side of the club, and, if

managed well, that should pay dividends in the medium to long term for the club.

6   Above all, we will try to rebuild the reputation of this football club.

I can bear witness that these were not false promises, and Boston United - on the day of my retirement-was again a well run club.

But Messrs Newton and Kempster will have been reminded that success on the field of play can be elusive. The team has done okay during their tenure although yet to reach the heights attained in previous times, but they know all about building foundations - and it is the foundations they have created at the football club that make more success possible. Certainly it is a far cry from the days when I thought the death knell was about to be rung at York Street.

It will be sad to leave York Street, but for the club to progress Chestnut Homes are providing a new community stadium

Seeds were sown

Little did I realise, that Friday evening in a Chinese restaurant near the International Centre in Bournemouth, that the seeds were being sown for the most tempestuous era in Boston United's history.

Maureen and I were on the south coast to represent the club at the annual meeting of the Southern Premier League where United's switch from the Northern Premier League was due to be rubber-stamped. After locating our hotel, we walked across the road to the restaurant for a meal. It was there that we met Steve Evans for the first time, along with his wife Sarah. He was manager of Stamford AFC and was representing them at the Southern League annual meeting and, in the evening, the dinner and presentation. Almost from the outset he was touting for the job as manager of The Pilgrims. From then onwards, he was telephoning me continually reminding me that he wanted the United job.

The opportunity arose when the popular Greg Fee resigned only a few games into the 1998/89 season. Steve continued to bombard me with 'phone calls when he heard the news. Eventually he arrived, unannounced, at our office in Spain Place seeking an interview with the board of directors. He had a meeting that morning with chairman Pat Malkinson, director Dick Carrington and myself. He certainly knew how to promote himself, and went away to submit an official application.

Steve was one of three applicants who were interviewed by the directors, the other two being Nicky Laws and John Ranshaw. Nicky was at Eastwood Town at the time, and is better known for his long association with Alfreton. John has managed at Kettering Town, Mansfield and Torquay.

Steve Evans gave a very confident interview and promised pretty well everything under the sun, and said he would bring in a lot of sponsorship and a lot of money. Even so, he did not impress all the directors some of whom preferred John Ranshaw. It was obvious, however, that the chairman was won over by Evans. Consequently, it was decided not to make a decision that night, but to "sleep on it".

Next morning, however, the chairman decided to appoint Steve Evans as the new manager of Boston United, against the wishes ofthe other directors.

And so began the reign of the controversial Scotsman, which was interrupted by a ban, but which took the club to playing heights supporters had only dreamed about.

It also brought controversy, heartache and, to this day, is still the subject of debate whenever United fans meet.

Over the years a number of different training venues have been used by the club. Jim Smith preferred the Grove Sports Centre, Balderton, near Newark, as it was more convenient for many of the players to get to evening training sessions .

Dave Cusack used the facilities at Haworth Colliery, near Blyth; Ray O'Brien and Arthur Mann chose Woolerton Park, near Nottingham. Some managers used Boston Grammar School.

The general trend was to take training to the players, rather than bring players to training . Without using the York Street pitch, which was not advisable because of the wear and tear, we did not have the facilities.

Things changed when players became full-time under Steve Evans' management . Somewhere was needed close to home for a training base. He chose the Princess Royal Sports Arena, at Wyberton Fen, commonly known locally as DABSI. Facilities there were excellent; good changing rooms, swimming pool, gym, weight room, running track and plenty of room for parking; but nowhere to play football! There was a grassed area, but no goalposts. The rest of the green space was given over to rugby, and Boston Rugby Club.

Nevertheless, it was decided that this could be the base, and the players could travel across town to use the excellent Freiston FC field at the Danny Flear Centre. It was a journey of about four miles each way and most of you reading this will know of the traffic problems in Boston, and the frustrating delays that can cause.

It was a particular headache when it came to delivering the players' lunches to PRSA. Jason and I were the couriers, and the fall-guys. It was a nightmare. Over a period of time there were a number of providers, including Zuccinis, the Italian restaurant in West Street, the Sandwich Shop in Main Ridge, Mick Wood's Country Gourmet Cafe in Pen Street, and Billinghams, near the New England Hotel.

Lunch on training days was usually scheduled for 1pm, and I transported the mainly hot food in my car, assisted by Jason. Sometimes the food was not ready. On other occasions I was caught in the heavy traffic, or it was the players who were held up. And it was not unusual for the manager to keep the players back, or change lunch time. You could hear the pasta splashing about as we drove.

At the stadium Jason and I had to serve the food, provide the drinks, clear up the dirty pots, and take the containers back to either the providers, or the ground, for washing up. Many times we would be late with this Meals on Wheels service, and often the players did not like the food provided. There were frequent rollickings from the mana ger. In fact, if we could escape without a row of some kind, we thought we had done well. It was a farce and took two hours out of my busy day, time I had to make up.

Eventually members of DABSI became fed up with us, and there came a parting of the ways. They did not like see players wandering about half naked, or using the gym and swimming pool when they were not paid-up members.

When the club was full-time some of the players lived locally in bed and breakfast establishments, or at the holiday flats at Lineside, Hubbert's Bridge. Some lived at Newark to save them travelling many miles home every day.

If we lost on a Saturday the manager was liable to call the players in for extra training on the Sunday morning, forcing them to travel from all over the country for an hour, probably more to inconvenience them rather than do any serious training . I was summoned to the training ground regularly, often many times a day, which interrupted my work on other important tasks. The turbulence was tolerated because the Evans' methods were bringing results, and giving the fans plenty to cheer about. They did not know how life was in the background. I doubt whether most of them would have cared anyway. They were enjoying the results and there is no doubt that Mr Evans was able to sweet-talk good players into signing for the club, and he knew how to turn them into a winning team. He was hell-bent on success, and Boston United's wins were victories for Steve Evans.

It was, of course, not rows all the time, and there were spells when I got on reasonably well with him, but it was a bit like walking on eggshells . If I am perfectly honest, I did not like his management style, not only with me but also with other staff, players and opposing clubs. On at least two occasions he reduced me to tears. Not a very manly thing for me to do, you may think, and I am sure he thought it was a w eakness, but the altercations were so stressful. There were times when I felt like walking away from it but, for better or worse, I stuck with it.

There was always controversy surrounding the man. His opinions were splashed across the local newspapers, and he appeared on Radio Lincolnshire almost as often as some of their regular presenters. His bullishness often stemmed any serious questioning of some of the things he was saying.

He walked hand in hand with trouble - confrontations with referees, the Football Association, Lincolnshire FA, the Conference, his own players, opposition managers ... the list was almost endless, and included people away from the game of football.

For instance, I had to handle complaints from two kennel owners that Steve's dogs had overstayed, by many weeks, the time for which they had been booked in. Both situations, I believe, were settled amicably.

For some of his time as manager of Boston United, Steve drove an eye-catching, sporty black car with a personalised BUFC number. It was very conspicuous, not least it seems because of the manner in which it was driven judging by the number of calls I received from other drivers alleging that they had been "inconvenienced" by this particular car. It caught the attention of the police, too, mainly for speeding on the road between Peterborough and Boston, and on one occasion Steve had to go to court to explain why he should not receive a driving ban because of the number of penalty points he had accrued. As ever, he must have had a plausible explanation because he escaped a ban!

Add to these escapades the FA fines and suspensions, altercations with referees and opposing teams, and you can see that life was never dull with Steve Evans around.

Despite what was going on in his life, including the dealings which eventually led to a criminal conviction and a lengthy ban from football, nothing seemed to distract him from continuing to plot the previously unheard of success of Boston United. It is a great pity that all this peripheral activity has distracted from his outstanding achievements results-wise, not only with Boston United but also with subsequent clubs.

Audacious and ambitious

The most audacious signing for United by Steve Evans was undoubtedly Paul Gascoigne, by general consensus one of the most talented footballers this country has known. His peak was long gone by the time he was tempted to York Street, and the sad story of his decline had been well documented, but he was still big news, and his arrival put United firmly in the national Press.

Paul Gascoigne

Not that the introductory Press conference arranged by Messrs Evans and Rodwell went to plan. Far from it. It was planned that Paul should meet the media at the Princess Royal Sports Arena (known as DABSI locally) at midday. There were about 30 reporters from television, radio and newspapers present, including Sky TV, BBC Look North and ITV's Calendar programmes.

About half an hour before the scheduled start I received a telephone call from Jim Rodwell asking me and Craig Singleton to go to the stadium to present Paul's apologies because he was ill and was unable to attend. It was a rush to get there in time, but that was not the end of the panic. At 12.45pm I received another call from Jim asking me to go to the New England Hotel to pick up Paul, and his dad John, and take them to Newark to catch the 2.10pm train to Newcastle. I dropped Craig off at the office and rushed to the New England where the poorly Paul was stretched out on a settee, obviously in pain. Paul had to lay across the front and back seat of the car, while his dad sat in the back. We were racing against time to catch the train and Paul was moaning and groaning all the way to Newark. We arrived with minutes to spare. John and I had to carry Paul onto the train, and load the luggage. When the train pulled out of the station I thought I would never see Paul again, he was so poorly.

Imagine my surprise when, two weeks later, he returned to Boston fit and well, and ready to play again. I could hardly believe my eyes. While in Boston, Paul stayed at the New England but spent a lot of time across the road at the Red Cow Hotel, especially when football was on television . He also spent time at the gymnasium at the Geoff Moulder Swimming Pool helping members, especially anyone who had an illness, with their exercises.

He played six times for United, four in Division Two, one in the League Cup against Fulham, and against Lincoln City in the County Cup. He did not do the amount of coaching I am sure he would have liked to have done. The players loved him, but I think the only conclusion you can reach is that he was brought to Boston as a publicity stunt. If that was the case, it certainly worked. I never knew how much he was paid, or where the money came from. I think that working with Steve Evans was a culture shock for even someone as much-travelled as Paul.

During his stay, the mail arriving at the club increased enormously. He had more than the club, and this included shirts, photographs, programmes and memorabilia which fans wanted signing. He signed a few each day and my wife, Maureen, posted them off for him.

The first day he arrived at the club, my daughter Lisa came to meet him as, when she was poorly in Great Ormond Street Hospital the BBC's legendary John Matson had visited her with a get-well card signed by Paul and Gary Lineker. She took the card to show him and thanked him for it. He was very kind to her and had a good chat.

During the short time he was at Boston he treated me and the staff very well, and it is sad to see reports, and photographs, of the struggles that have blighted the end of his career. I would love to see him again, if only to see what his memories were of his spell with Boston United. We have one reminder of him in our house. He gave Maureen his shirt before he departed.

As recently as November 2016, in an interview with Patrick Collins, of the Mail on Sunday, Paul spoke of signing for Boston United. "I went to Boston," he said. "That was a nightmare. I was sitting in me Dad's and we'd had a couple of drinks, then the phone goes, and a fellow says 'Hi Paul, d'you wanna sign for Boston? And I put me hand over the mouthpiece of the phone and said 'Right Dad, get your case packed, flip flops, the lot, we're going to Boston. "They gave me the directions and they told me to get off the train at such and such, and I said to Dad 'Ohs***, I think there's another Boston'. I didn't know about this one in Lincolnshire. Their chairman was a clever lad. He says 'Well Gazza, it'll be a nice few grand a week. Any crowd over 2,500, you'll get the money'. So I thought they'll get a full house if I play and I'll get decent wages. So I signed. Then I found it only held 2,250. So I shook the chairman's hand. I said 'That's class, that is.' I suppose I'm mad."

Nobody could ever accuse Steve Evans of under statement. He was always aiming big. Sometimes I felt that, in his own mind, he thought he was managing a Premier League club rather than little Boston United.

And so it was that he organised a few days away pre-season at the most palatial of venues, the Five Lakes at Tolleshunt Knights, Maidon, Essex. I was not in the party that travelled by Sleafordian Coaches, but a friendly fixture had been arranged at Braintree Town for the last day of the trip and I had to make arrangements for the coach to pick up the players, and take the kit for this match . I, and other members of staff, travelled on the coach driven by Kay Epton, and we arrived on time. We loaded up and had time to look around the magnificent facilities which included lots of top-class pitches, golf courses, and a superb hotel where the shirts of many famous clubs who had stayed there had been framed and adorned the walls of the hotel.

I don't know what, if anything, had gone wrong to upset the manager but he was in a foul mood on the journey to Braintree and he had a go at pretty well everyone on the coach, but especially the driver about being late and lost, in the most colourful lan guage. Kay was reduced to tears, and vowed that she would not drive the bus home. Luckily we were able to comfort her and she did bring us home, although it was a terrible journey after we had lost to Braint ree. The trip was reputed to have cost about £4,000, and I believe that it was possible because of the generosity of Michael Chinn who was a great benefactor of the club at the time.

Steve Evans and his long time assistant Paul Raynor

40

An earthquake that rocked foundations

It was a rumble that led to a massive earthquake which rocked the foundations of Boston Unit ed.

It was a Thursday. Date: May 23rd 2002. Time: 10am. I was working in the back room of the club's offices in Spain Place when I heard the front door open and someone talking to Maureen. He introduced himself as Graham Bean, Compliance Officer at the Football Association, and he asked to speak to a senior officer at the club.

Maureen called me in. I knew our visitor; I had spoken to him on numerous occasions in the past on other matters, but this time it was really serious. He showed me papers alleging that Boston United had broken FA rules and he wished to discuss the matter, in private, with the chairman or a senior director .

I contacted Pat Malkinson and we arranged to meet in the directors' room later that day. It was a meeting that lasted for several hours and it was a meeting destined to change the life of Boston United forever.

We were unaware that, at the same time, other investigators, ex-policemen working for Graham Bean, were calling on a number of United players who became w it nesses. At that moment in time The Pilgrims were on top of the world . A month earlier they had realised their dream of being promoted to the Football League when they clinched the Conference title by goal difference after a season-long battle with Dagenham and Redbridge. Although they went on to enjoy a five-year stay in the Football League, the eventual decline and battle against extinction can be traced to events that led to that meeting.

Graham Bean was accompanied by FA financial expert Jamie McGraw as they trawled through United's books and, as a result of what they saw - or, rather, did not see - they went away to formulate charges against manager Steve Evans, the man who had masterminded the Cinderella story of The Pilgrims modern-day progress, and chairman Pat Malkinson, who had seen the dream of his father realised after a spectacular rise in results over a four-year period .

The charges which eventually emerged were against two people - the manager and the chairman -and they alleged the submission of false contracts for players to the FA. Six players were found to have been paid more than the submitted contracts had shown.

It transpired that the players signed three contracts and only two of these were given to the club. One was sent to the FA and another was retained by the club.

These were different from the third one which was for the players' and manager's eyes only, and contained the true terms agreed. All were filled in by the manager.

For these financial irregularities, the club was docked four points and fined £100, 000.

This was announced in July 2002, but there were other hearings into allegations that attempts had been made to impede the inquiry by trying to silence one player-witness, Jim Dick, by bribing him with £8, 000 in cash.

For this Steve Evans - by this stage he had quit as manager after earlier being suspended by the club - was fined £8,000 and banned from football for 20 mont hs.

The ex-chairman, Pat Malkinson who had resigned as a director of the club, was fined £5, 250 and banned for 13 months.

The media labelled this episode "a scandal" as it hit the national, as well as local, headlines. At the end of the inquiries, Graham Bean was quoted as saying: "The sad thing about this whole story is that at the greatest moment in Boston's history, one man did so much to damage the club's reputation. In everything that went wrong at the club, Steve Evans was the common denominator."

Simon Hart, in a major article in the Sunday Telegraph, explained what the FA investigating team discovered: "Evans would routinely write out a contract for a footballer, which the player signed, and he would then ask the player to sign two other blank contracts, saying he would fill them out later to save time. The suspicion was that the two blank contracts were then filled out with lower figures without the players' knowledge. These were then passed to Blackwell, an innocent party in the deception, who retained one of them, and lodged the other with the FA."

Even now, as I recall this dark time in the history of the club, I have a sickening feeling to think that it was going on without me knowing anything about it. To this day, I do not know how the "unofficial" money was being paid to the players, and where it came fr om . But I became caught up in the intrigue when the Inland Revenue was made aware of what was happening and proceeded to allege that five of us at the club had conspired to defraud them of tax that should have been paid on these inflated wages.

That, as the court later decreed, dragged three innocent people into a story which Graham Bean described as "one to make your hairs stand on end." No action was taken against the players involved. I can only assume that they received re-adjusted tax demands.

As I have spoken to fans over the subsequent years I have found that there are still divided opinions on this issue. Some think that Boston United were doing nothing that other clubs must have done over the years, paying a little under the counter, a few back-handers so to speak.

Others are appalled at what was going on, and how it so nearly brought the club crashing to its deat h. I know it led to me having lots of sleepless nights .

Following in the footsteps of criminals

When, in 1970, Jim Smith knocked at my door and asked me to help out at Boston United, I did not have in mind following in the footsteps of the notorious Kray twins, nor did I envisage treading the trail that took wife killer Dr Crippen and Nazi propaganda broadcaster William Joyce (Lord Haw Haw) towards the gallows.

Yet, here I was, gut-wrenchingly nervous, entering England's most famous magistrates' court in Bow Street, London, just as they had once done. The thousands of accused who had been part of this now-closed court's 266-year history must have suffered a variety of emotions. None could have been more anxious, more scared, more uncertain of what was held in store during the coming weeks. In my worst nightmare I could never imagine that this was happening. None of this was in my job description.

I was there by invitation, almost. By summons, actually. Her Majesty's Inland Revenue had sent an innocuous-looking letter by recorded delivery with the shattering news that I was required to attend court to answer charges that I had committed the offence of, along with Patrick Malkinson, Brian James, Ian Lee and Stephen Evans, "conspiring together to cheat the Public Revenue by dishonestly failing to declare the true Pay As You Earn Income Tax and Class 1 National Insurance liability of Boston Football Club Limited for the years 1997 to 2001 inclusive."

I was frightened. I knew I had done nothing wrong. That made it even more scary. My life was turned upside down by the arrival of that letter. My family was in turmoil. The letter elaborated on the charge by claiming that we were all party to:

1   Submitting, or causing to be submitted, false year end P35 employer's
     annual returns.

2   Recording, or causing to be recorded, on the company payroll football
     players' and other employees' wages as expenses.

3   Failure to record on the company payroll payments to players namely (a)
     signing on fees; (b) bonus payments.

4   Registering, or causing to be registered, with theFootball Association
     player contracts containing false details as to remuneration.

It was alleged that the Public Revenue had been cheated out of £282,446 over a four-year period. I knew that I had done nothing wrong, but what if the court thought otherwise?

On the day of that first hearing - Friday September 30th 2005 - I drove Pat and Brian to Steve Evans' house in Eye, and then we went to London by train from Peterborough, travelled across London and met up with Ian at the court.

Reporters from our local newspapers, and television companies were waiting for the hearing. We were all searched. and called into the dock to listen to the charges that the Inland Revenue said we must answer.

It was all over in about 15 minutes- but it was just the beginning of the ordeal. We were all committed for trial at Southwark Crown Court at a later date. The story hit the newspaper headlines and the airwaves, and was all the talk in football circles. Not at all pleasant. Then came the wait, first for the date of the trial, and then for the trial itself. It was impossible to get it all out of your mind. I tried to carry on working as normally as I could, but it was a very stressful time and there were the constant distractions of meetings with solicitors and barristers as they prepared my defence.

Ringrose Law were my family solicitors, but they felt that they could not represent me as they had already been engaged by Steve Evans, but they found me alternative solicitors, Bird and Co, at Grantham. It was from this office that Stuart Wild agreed to represent me, and he took me to see London barrister, Richard Latham. Stuart was brilliant throughout, supportive, friendly and re-assuring. I could not have wished for anyone better to represent me. Richard had said, from the moment he read the papers relating to the trial, that I should never have been part of it. That was nice to hear and I prayed that the judge would have the same opinion.

The build-up to the trial was agonising, not only for me but also for Maureen and the girls. As D-Day arrived they travelled with me to Stuart Wild's home at Quadring on the Sunday afternoon before the trial was due to start the following day. Emotions were running high as we said goodbye to the family, and to Stuart's wife, Linda, to drive to Peterborough before travelling by train to King's Cross. Stuart had arranged for us to stay at a hotel near the Houses of Parliament and the Big Wheel and, as a distraction and, no doubt, in a bid to settle my nerves, he took me for a walk around London.

It was an early start the following day as we had to meet Richard Latham, and another barrister, Gary Summers, before the hearing commenced at Southwark Crown Court. Again there was the humiliating search, and the worrying sight of prison vans arriving with "clients" for the day's activities. The local media was there in force, but this was a hearing that was destined to interest a wider audience.

Southwark Crown Court is housed in a massive building and was a reminder that I was way out of my comfort zone in the Big City, such a contrast to little old Boston. If memory serves me right, we were in Court No 13 and, after all the preliminaries, all five of us were ushered into the dock behind glass protection.

Little did I know at this stage that I would be there for another three and a half weeks, and that the only time I would be asked to speak would be to give my name, and date of birth, at the very outset of the trial.

Later in that first day, Steve Evans entered a plea of guilty and was allowed to go home, on bail, until the end of the trial.

When the court adjourned for the day, we had another walk around the city- I was becoming familiar with the sounds and sights of London - and, on arrival back at the hotel, was surprised to see the familiar face of Graham Bean, the Football Association Compliance Officer whose visit to York Street had set this legal ball rolling, booking in for the night. He was due to give evidence at the trial the following day.

During the second day there was the shock revelation that Pat Malkinson was also pleading guilty, and he, too, was released on bail, leaving just the three of us - Brian James, Ian Lees and myself-to continue facing trial.

That evening we had to move hotels as the one where we had been was fully booked. This time Stuart and I had to go our separate ways. I moved into a hotel near the court but I had a companion, because that was where Brian James was staying. I now had only a 200-yard walk to court. We came home on Friday evenings as the trial continued, and returned to London on Sunday, but at one stage there was a midweek break when the judge adjourned the hearing at 1pm on Wednesday-the very day when United had a match against Lincoln City.

I could not resist the temptation of returning home to carry out my normal match day duties. I arranged for one of the work experience inmates of North Sea Camp to drive my car to Peterborough to pick me up along with Stuart. On reflection since it seems rather incongruous- a serving prisoner fetching us home from an on-going trial. But he was there waiting for us as we arrived at Peterborough station at about 4pm, and drove us home.

I ran the match, stayed at the ground until the early hours of the morning to catch up with my work, went home to snatch a brief sleep before getting up at Sam to drive back to Peterborough, accompanied by long-suffering Maureen, to catch an early train so that I could be back at Southwark Crown Court for the resumption of the trial at 10.30am. The train was scheduled to arrive in London at 8.30am. Well, that was the plan. But, to my horror, the train came to a halt at St Neots, and it did not move. It was going nowhere because a technical problem on the line was preventing trains from entering London. Passengers mingled on the platform, some more agitated than others, but none more so than me. I pictured myself being thrown into the cells if I was late for the re-start of the trial. Stuart was not with me; he was back in his office at Grant ham , and had arranged for a stand-in to represent me that day.

I could not contact the court to make them aware of my predicament and, while I was pondering on my next move, I bumped into a well-known official, Neale Barry, Head of the Referees' Department, who was on his way to the Football Association headquarters, and shared my woes with him. Finally, at around 9am, we received the news that an attempt was to be made to take the train into King's Cross station, and we finally arrived there at about 10am. I jumped into a taxi which got me to court with about five minutes to spare, only to be told that the start of the trial would be delayed because witnesses travelling from Yorkshire and Lincolnshire had been held up by the same problem as me! All that panic had been unnecessary.

The hearing re-started after lunch when most of the witnesses were ex-Boston United players. Conditions improved a little for the three of us on trial when the judge decided that we were no threat to anyone and it was not essential for us to be holed up in the dock, behind glass. We could sit in the body of the court. I continued my silent vigil until into the third week when my QC, Richard Latham told me that he was going to make a submission to the judge that I had no case to answer. Brian James' representative made a similar plea. It took all afternoon, and we had to wait overnight for the verdict. It was bad news for Brian. He had to continue with the trial.

Basically my defence was that, although I signed documents, I only did so under instructions from the club accountant, or the board. Any player contracts I completed were as directed by the club chairman or manager. On occasions I helped players to complete mileage forms but, in these cases, payments made were genuine expenses. My barrister made an impassioned, and eloquent, plea that I was only doing what I was instructed to do, and in no way instigated any of the alleged off ences. I had to wait on tenterhooks for an hour or more as the judge summed up the case as it applied to me. At the end of this agonising wait- relief. I was free to leave the court. Judge Andrew Goymer had ruled that I had no case to answer. He ruled that "the state of the evidence as far as John Blackwell is concerned is such that a jury could not draw the conclusion that he was part of the conspiracy set out in the indictment."

I was walking on air, and could not wait to telephone the good news to Maureen, and my good friend, Fran Martin, secretary at Lincoln Cit y. After a quick celebratory drink with my legal team, and a dash to the hotel to collect my belongings, I arranged to meet Stuart Wild at King's Cross station for our journey home. There was just one final problem to overcome. My ticket was to Peterborough, Stuart's was to Grantham where he had left his car.

I decided to travel with him to Grantham but, on arrival there, I was stopped by the guard and I had to pay for the extra miles on the train journey. I was happy to admit to that "crime." At Grantham I met up with former United director, Stuart Bateman, who had been to London on business . Stuart Wild drove us both to the Supreme Inn, at Bicker, where Maureen had arranged to meet me, and she drove us both back to Boston. The nightmare of the trial was over for me. Or so I thought, but it had one last kick in the teeth.

The next day I went in to work to continue my normal duties only to be greeted by the shocking news from Chief Executive, Jim Rodwell, that I was to be suspended. I was furious. It seemed that he was handing out his own form of justice, and it differed from the verdict of the judge at Southwark Crown Court.

However, I had the last laugh. Towards the end of the week, Jim came round to my house cap in hand, obviously having realised that there was no-one to run the weekend game, to ask me to return to carry out my usual match day duties. Some would have been appalled at the hypocrisy of it all, but I was just pleased to get back to normality.

Later, I reflected on the fact that Jim Rodwell was reported in the newspapers as saying that the man who was the heartbeat of these offences, Steve Evans, "deserved the chance to manage in the Football League" when he returned to the club after his suspension . Yet the man who was found to have no case to answer was told the stay away from the club while the trial continued - until, that is, it was realised he was needed. I will leave you to make of that what you will!

Meanw hile , Brian James and Ian Lees had to endure another week of the trial before they were found not guilty. Some time later Steve Evans and Pat Malkinson were called to receive their sentences. Pat Malkinson, in poor health at the time, was given a two-year prison sentence, suspended for two years, and ordered to pay £323,444 back tax, and interest , to the Inland Revenue, and had his gaming licence taken away. Steve Evans was sentenced to 12 months in prison, suspended for two years, and ordered to pay £1,000 costs.

Judge Goymer said that the normal punishment for such a "sustained and considerable fraud" would be a prison sentence, but he felt that there were exceptional circumstances for both defendants which meant that he could suspend those sentences. He took into account the fact that neither had gained personally from the fraud, and Steve Evans had also been punished by the Football Association.

It had been a harrowing time for all concerned, and a sad episode in the history of Boston United. Although I had been given legal aid, and awarded costs, I was still heavily out of pocket and family savings had taken a big hit. In addition the emotional cost had been draining. When the verdict became known, I was inundated with telephone calls and messages of goodwill, all of which were reassuring. I am told that social media was also awash with comments welcoming the out come. I will always treasure the memories of those people who took the trouble to write, or call. They will never know how much it meant to me.

Day a dream came true

The West London town of Hayes will be forever a milestone in the history of Boston United. It was there that The Pilgrims realised their dream of achieving Football League status by clinching the Conference championship with a 2-0 win.

It was a Sunday, the last day of the 2001-02 season. Arch rivals Dagenham and Redbridge were also playing. The two teams were level on points, but if we won, the championship was ours. In that case it did not matter what Dagenham did; we had the better goal difference. In the event, they beat Chester 3-0, a result which would have given them the title had we slipped up.

Both teams finished on 84 points from their 42 games. United had been beaten eight times, and Dagenham had lost only six games- but they had drawn 12 times, while United had been level at the final whistle on nine occasions. The crucial difference was that United had scored 84 goals and conceded 42, having the most prolific attack and the meanest defence in the league, while Dagenham had scored 70 goals and conceded 47 times. The two clubs were 14 points clear of third-placed Yeovil.

United prepared for this all-or-nothing-game by staying overnight at the Holiday Inn at Wycombe and training locally. When we left the hotel on Sunday morning, for the 45-minute journey to the Hayes ground, we could not believe how many Boston supporters were making their way to the match, all eager to experience that "I was there" moment as they anticipated an history-making day. It was an unbelievable experience and, on arrival at the ground, it was a sea of black and amber, very few Hayes supporters bothering to turn out. The official attendance was 3, 249, and most of them must have been from Boston.

Hayes had been involved in a relegation battle and, in fact, did go down after finishing third from bottom. Clearly, the form book said that United were firm favourites, but the difference in league placings would count for nothing with so much at stake, and with tension running high. Yes, tension really was running high that day, but Simon Weatherstone's goal after just five minutes did ease the nerves a little, but anxiety returned when midfielder Peter Costello was sent off, for a second bookable offence, in the 46th minute.

Simon Rusk, Paul Bastock, Jamie Gould, Mark Angel & Mark Clifford celebrate promotion to The Football League

Manager Steve Evans' response was to bring substitute Ray Warburton on in the place of Neil Tarrant in midfield, and Warburton rewarded the manager with a headed goal in the 49th minute to settle things down and play his part in a second promotion from the Conference in successive seasons, having played for previous year's champions Rushden and Diamonds. The substitution was hailed as a masterstroke by the fans to whom Evans had become a hero.

He enjoyed the moment, perhaps even more than the players who were treated to an extra night's stay at the Wycombe hotel to celebrate the promotion-winning season.

The team that day w as: Bastock, Clifford, Rodwell, Ellender, Gould, Rusk (Lodge 9), S Weatherstone, Costello, Angel, Clare (Elding 89), Tarrant (Warburton 48); subs not used: Cook, Conroy (gk).

To put the icing on the cake, Daryl Clare, with 25 goals, had finished as top scorer in the Conference.

Other staff - me included - travelled back to Boston with the kit and to make arrangements for the team, with trophy, to return to Boston the following evening.

The Social Club was packed with supporters waiting for us to arrive, and the next evening the York Street ground was full of fans waiting to greet the triumphant team.

It was, remarkably, an achievement predicted by Steve Evans early in his term as United manager, and after that incredible first season when he steered the team from relegation candidates to promotion from the Dr Martens League as runners-up to Nuneaton, after which he sai d: "I think everyone at the club can be proud of what has been achieved in a relatively short space of time. "After a few weeks in the job I went on record as saying I felt we could finish as at least runners-up, and I am delighted. "But this is just the starting point . The hard work now begins to identify, and bring in, the extra quality signings I feel will be necessary to give us a championship chance next season." His confidence had proved well founded.

An elated Pat Malkinson, on the verge of handing the club over to Des Wood, said: "We are lucky to have Steve as our manager . He has transformed the club virtually single-handed, and one day he will be a Premiership manager, I am sure of that."

Less enamoured by Boston's joy was Dagenham's boss Garry Hill who insisted that he would not be congratulating Steve Evans. The two had been involved in a war of words over the season. Hill was quoted as saying: "Missing out is hard for us to accept because we got 84 points, averaged two points a game and lost fewer games than any other club . "But I think we've made a good case for the Conference in their bid to win another promotion place."

Evans, however, could not forget what he regarded as Dagenham's disrespectful lap of honour after they had beaten United and gone seven points clear at the top of the table. "I have only ever known of laps of honour from teams who have won championships, or cups, not teams who have won just one game. "We are champions, and now my players have gone on a real lap of honour. There has been rivalry, but I respect Dagenham and what they have been striving for."

United player-coach , Neil Thompson, had some praise for his manager when he said: "These are moments to be treasured. We have a good set of lads and Steve Evans is good at creating promotion teams, but Dagenham must be devastated to miss out on goal difference."

Life, however, had never been better for Boston United. There was not a cloud in the sky. No-one could rain on this Boston Tea Party. Or could they? Not, surely, the man who had engineered the success that had been dreamed about for so long? The man who had lifted the club out of the doldrums? The man who had picked Boston United up by the scruff of the neck and shaken it into life? The man who had flavoured often outrageous behaviour with astute signings and brave footballing decisions?

United fans had entered the summer of 2002 with a spring in their steps, but the clouds gathered as it emerged that Football Association representatives had visited the club, searched the books and found evidence that resulted in a £100, 000 fine and four points deduction for contract irregularities.

The party-mood was brought to an abrupt end. It was raining cats and dogs now.

Long-serving chairman, Pat Malkinson, had already handed over the running of the club to businessmen Des Wood and Trevor Killick who had suspended the manager while the inquiry was ongoing. Subsequently, the FA imposed a 14-month ban on Steve Evans who was revealed to be the architect of the wrongdo ing. Yes, the man who had given the club that incredible kiss of life, had, in fact in my opinion, given it a near-fatal stab in the back.

Former chairman, Pat Malkinson, had also been banned from the game , but it was Evans who bore the brunt of the furore from the Press, erstwhile admiring supporters, and high ranking off icials. "Because I have been charged, it doesn't mean I am guilty," he protest ed. I have been advised not to comment on the charges I face, so all I can say is that I am spending more time on the issue, preparing for when I stand in front of the FA.

"I was saddened and disappointed when I heard and, in all respects, these words are two huge understatements."

Dagenham saw this Boston bombshell as a glimmer of hope that they, and not The Pilgrims, might now be promoted to the Football League. This hope was voiced by their chairman Dave Andrews when he said: "If there is any justice in football, we should be going up into the Football League as champions of the Conference if- and I repeat if- Boston are guilty of these charges."

The only little ray of sunshine to emerge was that, yes, Boston United would be allowed to take their hard-won place in League Two . That news was a big relief at a time when it seemed to me that the whole of the football world seemed to be against the club. Boston United were labelled "cheats" and Dagenham and Redbridge were campaigning hard for the title to be taken away from us. They felt that they should become the promoted club.

The FA decision that we were clear to take our place in the Football League did not come until the middle of July and that left us with precious little time to prepare for the new season. In fact our first ever League Two game was only three weeks away. It was scheduled to be against AFC Bournemouth who had experienced their own troubles which had seen them plunge down the rungs of the Football League ladder. Their later success was something even t heir most ardent supporter could not dare to dream about . Nevertheless, they were big opponents to us, and I wanted everything to go well on the day.

We had Porta Cabins brought onto the car park to provide much-needed office space and what would have normally been three months' preparation was condensed into three weeks. At times it was all a bit chaotic and I shall always be grateful for the advice that was readily available from Lincoln City secretary, Fran Martin, who proved to be a real friend in our hour of need.

There was a lot of catching up to do, and I remember explaining all this to Grahame Lloyd, a writer who was researching his book comparing life at York Street with that at Lincoln Cit y's Sincil Bank . The book was called One Hell of a Season, Imps, Pilgrims and Tales of the Unexpected.

The FA investigation had frightened off some players from joining the club and it was not until we knew the outcome of this that we could prepare contracts, with quite a few having to be changed from non-League to Football League status. The hefty £100, 000 fine was a big blow, and the four-point deduction was a deterrent to some players.

Nevertheless, acting manager Neil Thompson, whose quality coaching had played an important part in the promotion push, contrived to get a team together, and pre-season practice matches went ahead. There was just a handful of us working behind the scenes on the administrative side but, although not everything was as I would have liked it for that first game, we just about managed.

Steve Evans, who had made all this possible, had resigned by the time the Bournemouth match came along, so was never able to enjoy the fruits of his labour.

Neil Thompson was now officially team manager.

The day before the opening game, ex-chairman Pat Malkinson put aside the woes that had enveloped him, to pay a visit to my temporary office. "I know that you are going to be busy tomorrow, John," he said. "But make sure that you go in and see the start of the game." I took his advice, and stood near the tunnel to see the kick-off to Boston United's first game in the Football League. I am pleased I did because it was a very special moment, one that can never be repeated.

I have never worked so hard in my life as I did in those three weeks of preparation. There was a lot of Press interest in our Football League debut, and I was followed throughout the day by Mark Clemitt, of the BBC Five Live radio programme, prior to, during and after the match. The stress of it all eventually reduced me to tears. It was such an emotional day, but quite satisfying that the game ended in a 2-2 draw, although it left us still three points adrift of the teams that were beaten that day.

I remember, later, describing the day to Grahame Lloyd. "I went in at 7am on the day of the match," I told him, "and I didn't know where I was, and I made a few mistakes.

"It was very busy - more hectic than I expected, and it got on top of me. It was shocking and we had a few teething troubles. Even though people were milling around from about midday, there were long queues at the turnstiles, but we managed to get everybody in by eight minutes past three. A few programme and golden ticket sellers did not turn up so it was hard work.

"The organisation wasn't quite right, but I think we did reasonably well. I didn't see any of the goals but I understand that it was a good game."

There were something like 500 orders for our matchday programme, as well as many more wanting fixture cards and team sheets as mementoes. At least, and with great relief, our life in the Football League was on its way. There was a little respite from the hurly burly of organising a home game as our next three matches were away at Hartlepool, Wrexham and Bristol Rovers, this latter one being our debut in the League Cup. If nothing else it reminded us of the travelling involved.

The next big test for our administration was the home game against county rivals Lincoln City.

Agonising welcome

As boardroom welcomes go, this was a bit of a shocker and I was left on the ground writhing in agony and gasping for breath!

I couldn't believe what had just happened. We were at Underhill, the old home of Barnet Football Club, one of The Pilgrims' keenest rivals over the years in non-League and Football League. United had snatched a 1-0 victory with a late goal in a hard-fought game and, as usual, I made my way to the Barnet boardroom to socialise with the home club's officials. I went to shake hands with Stan Flashman, the so-called King of the Ticket Touts at the time, who was chairman of Barnet. His response was anything but friendly. He aimed a kick right between my legs, and he was much more accurate than the home forwards had been during the game. He was bang on target, and the reminder was there for days through discoloration and tenderness!

It was a bit like a nightmare. Sometimes you wake up and wonder if it ever happened. The Pilgrim party were aghast at this behaviour, and refused to go into the boardroom, leaving the ground as soon as possible. The next morning the 'phone rang at work. It was Stan Flashman, apologising. "I shouldn't have done it. I was so angry that we had been beaten," he said. Too right, he shouldn't have done it, but I accepted his apology. I know many people would not have done so.

So much has happened since those halcyon days, but none of the fall-out since the FA Inquiry and court cases can alter the fact that, yes, for five memorable seasons, the Pilgrims were on the first ladder of football's elite. Many fans, countrywide, realised for the first time where the town was situated. The name appeared on televised results throughout the season. Boston was on the map more than it had ever been before thanks to the football club.

None of the debris we have waded through in subsequent years can take away those memories and experiences which I dare not even dream about when setting out in football administration all those years ago with Real Towell and Towell FC. And there could be no bigger contrast between playing on some of the grounds in rural Lincolnshire, some nothing more than farmers' fields, and the stadiums of clubs even on the bottom rung of the Football League ladder. Some of these venues are now the homes of Premier League clubs.

Standards, we found, both on and off the pitch, were higher than we had ever experienced before but, despite having four points deducted at the very start of our first season, Boston United survived at this level longer than many had predicted - and longer than some had hoped.

Neil Thompson was the manager when we played our first Division Three games in season 2002-03 after the man who guided us to promotion, Steve Evans, was banned from football for 20 mont hs. United actually earned 58 points on the pitch that season, but the final league table showed that we had 54, having been deducted four points before we even started as a result of much publicised demeanours.

So that was a satisfactory start with 15 wins and 13 draws from our 46 games, scoring 55 goals and conceding 56. Richard Logan was top scorer with ten goals.

The next season, partly under the guidance of Neil Thomson and partly under the controversially returning Steve Evans, saw an improvement with an 11th place finish, albeit with only one more point than was actually earned in the first campaign.

Full record for 2003-04 was Played 46 Won 16 Drawn 11 Lost 19 Goals For 50, Goals Against 54, Pts 59. The seven goals Neil Redfearn scored made him top scorer.

The third season, with Steve Evans fully restored as manager, saw United total only one point less but that also meant a drop to 16th, although it was the first time at this level - now named League Two - that we scored more goals than we conceded, thanks to a 20-goal contribution from Andy Kirk. End of season record, showing the fewest wins so far, read as fol low s: P46 W14 D16 L16 F62 A58 Pts 58.

Highest points tally of Unit ed's Football League reign came in 2005-06 when they finished 11th with 60 points with a middle-of-the-road record of P46 W15D16 L15 F62 A50 Pts 60. Julian Joachim top-scored with 16 goals.

Then came the season we all dreaded, and relegation from the Football League with a miserable total of 36 points from the 46 games, and only 12 wins compared to 24 defeats. Defensive weaknesses were highlighted by the 80 goals conceded, and 51 scored. Drewe Broughton needed only eight goals to make him top scorer.

Attendances over the five-year stay at this level highlighted the gradual decline of performances on the field of play, as the average went downwards as follows: 3049, 2960, 2932, 2519 and 2152. The statistics tell only part of the story and do not reveal the excitement and enjoyment I, and I am sure most supporters, had from this new experience. Nothing can take that away from us.

There was, for instance, all the local Derby fixtures against Lincoln City, Scunthorpe United and Grimsby Town, hitherto restricted to county cup competitions when we were simply regarded as nuisance underdogs. Now we were competing on equal terms, having won the right to be in the same league.

There were other matches which almost fell into the local Derby category, certainly it was within easy reach for travelling fans to follow the Pilgrims to places like Mansfield Town, Notts County, Hull City, Peterborough United, Cambridge United and Rushden and Diamonds - a contrast to the long journeys to Bournemouth, Hartlepool and Wrexham for example.

Our first home Boxing Day fixture against Lincoln City was a full house, and we tried to make it an extra special day by adding to the Christmas atmosphere with Santa Claus riding around the pitch on the club mower. Father Christmas for the day was club steward Graham Late. There were 2,050 visiting supporters packed into the Town End.

All visiting clubs brought a sizeable number of their own fans which must have given a boost to the Boston economy.

Many referees who later became household names cut their teeth on League Two and Division Three soccer at that time, people like Lee Mason, Anthony Taylor, Kevin Friend, Andre Marriner, Martin Atkinson, Johnathan Moss, Neil Swarbrick and Graham Poll being among them.

Among the famous old grounds we visited were: Boothferry Park (Hull City), Bootham Crescent (York City}, Haigh Avenue (Southport}, Plainmoor (Torquay United), Racecourse Ground (Wrexham), Aggborough (Kidderminster Harriers), Edgeley Park (Stockport County), Underhill Stadium (Barnet), Gigg Lane (Bury), Blundell Park (Grimsby Town), Edgar Street (Hereford United), Sincil Bank (Lincoln City}, Gay Meadow (Shrewsbury Town}, County Ground (Swindon}, Bescot Stadium (Walsall}, Adams Park (Wycombe Wanderers), Rootes Hall (Southend United), Brunton Park (Carlisle) and Brisbane Road (Leyton Orient).

We were also early visitors to some of the new grounds coming onto the circuit, at places such as Hull, Huddersfield, Northampton, Darlington and Milton Keynes. Who knows, maybe United will be playing at a new ground the next time they are in the Football League.

On our first League visit to Leyton Orient (I say League visit because I am mindful of the fact that Don Donovan took United there for a FA Cup replay many years earlier) we were invited to lunch with Orient chairman, snooker and darts Supremo, Barry Hearn, and snooker star Steve Davis MBE.

Gaining promotion to the Football League enabled United to embark on another adventure, and that was competing in the League Cup and testing our growing status against even better teams.

Our first venture at this level was soon after our baptism to League Two when we made the long journey to Bristol Rovers and came away with a meritorious 2-0 win thanks to goals from Burton and Simon Weatherstone. We took another step up in class in the next round, and that proved too big a task as we were beaten 5-1 by Cardiff City, Paul Ellender being our scorer.

The next season we were drawn at home twice, first against Luton Town whom we beat in a 4-3 thriller, with the Boston goals coming from Courtney Pitt, Jason Lee and Lee Thompson (2).

This gave United a York Street tie against Fulham. I remember the Londoners' players and officials flew to Lincolnshire, landing at RAF Coningsby ready to be picked up by their coach which had travelled up with the kit in the afternoon. After the game, the 'bus took them back to the RAF station, returned to York Street to pick up the kit, and then headed back to London down the A1.

Lee Beevers scored United's goal in a 5-1 defeat, and that was the last goal United netted in the League Cup, but there was still honour in two 1-0 away defeats in the following two seasons against the "big boys" of Sheffield United (season 2005-06) and Brighton and Hove Albion (2006-07). Many of these clubs have travelled in a completely different direction to United since those heady days.

There seemed to be a revolving door policy as far as players were concerned in the League Two days, an average of 40 different individuals wearing United colours each season. Some of the stays were so brief that I doubt whether the players concerned would be able to find their way back to York St reet. But there were also some very good players who became regulars, and big favourites with thefans.

There was never any question that Steve Evans was able to root out players who could do a good job for him and the team, and that talent never left him as subsequently he experienced management at Crawley, Rotherham United, Leeds United and Mansfield Town.

Games against other county teams were the highlight for many, and it gave supporters tremendous pleasure when our first-ever Football League win was at home to Lincoln City in front of a crowd of 5,159 packed into York St reet. Simon Weatherstone and Daryl Clare grabbed goals that sent Pilgrims fans home happy on that satisfying day, August 24th 2002 .

On the first day of the next year the two teams met again, and United held the Imps to a 1-1 draw before 7,846 fans at Sincil Bank, Richard Logan scoring United's precious goal. It is interesting to note that not until their tremendous championship winning season, enhanced by cup giantkilling, did the Lincoln attendances reach the levels of those matches against Boston United .

The games between the two clubs were usually close. We lost 1-0 at Lincoln on the Boxing Day of our second season, and drew 1-1 in the return game. Respective attendances in these games were 5,708 and 7,114.

In the third season United drew 2-2 at Sincil Bank in front of 7,142 fans, but lost the February night return 2-0, although again there was an excellent attendance of 6,445.

United earned the bragging rights in the fourth series of matches, drawing 0-0 at Lincoln (attendance 7,077 on Boxing Day) and winning 2-1 in the return which was played in March in front of a crowd of 4,476, Joachim and Duffield scoring the vital goals.

Honours were shared in United's final season of League Two football, the Pilgrims winning 1-0 at home and losing 1-2 away. The September midweek match at York Street saw the attendance down to 4,327, but there was another good crowd of 6, 820 for the Boxing Day return.

United never managed to beat Grimsby in a Football League fixture, drawing three of their six encounters, and losing the rest, including a 6-0 humiliation in the last of these matches. Again there were healthy attendances, especially at Grimsby, but rivalry never quite reached the fever pitch it was with Lincoln.

United also played Scunthorpe United six times in League games, winning three and losing only one.

All four of these county teams suffered relegation from League Two, but three of them bounced back, leaving United all alone and floundering after a double demotion.

One of the long journeys was to Carlisle, and I remember facing a dilemma after one game when our coach broke dow n. The Carlisle pitch had been flooded a week or so earlier but had drained sufficiently well for the game to be given the go-ahead . We stayed overnight at the Lakes Hotel, Penrith. After breakfast on match day, I and other members of staff took the kit to the ground, and then returned for the players nearer kick-off time. There were no problems with the coach. After the match we loaded the kit back onto the coach and were all set for the journey home. But the 'bus would not sta rt . Not a hint from the engine that it was going to come to life. So what do we do? After long discussions with Sleafordian Coaches, and driver Keith Taylor, it was arranged to borrow Carlisle United's team coach to take us back to Boston. Fortunately, Carlisle had a Tuesday fixture at Lincoln City and, after our coach had been repaired, they were able to bring it back to Lincolnshire, and return in their own coach. Problem solved .

Another long journey was to Swansea, requiring an overnight stay after the match. One I recall was on a Friday evening, a very important league fixture with both clubs too close to the wrong end of the table for comfort. It was at Swansea's famous old Vetch Field stadium, next to a prison, and was packed to the rafters for this relegation batt le. It was a tight, fraught encounter which eventually ended in a 0-0 draw, despite the fact that United ended the game with only nine men. Stuart Douglas and Tony Bennett were both sent off, but the remaining players battled hard to earn a vital point.

The following year we again played there in midweek, again in front of an almost full house, but lost 3-1. These two games come to mind as an illustration of how things can change so dramatically, and so quickly, in football.

As I was writing this, the Swans were again in a relegation battle, but this time from the Premier League, and at their new Liberty Stadium! And United had only just avoided a relegation fight in the National League North.

Since retirement I have been scouting for Swansea, and have very much enjoyed renewing acquaintances in non-League football as I search for players who might be capable of a move up the soccer ladder . There is a lot of talent at this level of the game. Secretary at Swansea in United's League days was Jackie Rockey, who became a good friend. She is still there 15 years on .

Of course, the one game that will remain forever in my memory, is our last one in the Football League- at Wrexham. A sad, sad occasion.

Wrexham players celebrate staying in The Football League whilst the Boston United players look on in despair at their relegation

Pilgrim fans, of course, were desperate for their team to survive the drop, and travelled in their hundreds, to make their voices heard in the bumper crowd of 13,000 jammed into the Racecourse Ground. Wrexham fans, too, were desperate to see their own team win this vital relegation battle.

While United supporters travelled across to Wales in convoys of coaches, the team and support staff travelled on the Friday morning to stay overnight at one of the best hotels I have ever experienced, the Carden Park in Cheshire.

Light training on Friday afternoon prepared the way for the do-or-die battle the following day. Optimism was high when we took the lead, but tears were flowing by the end as Wrexham grabbed three late goals to send United plummeting down the soccer ladder straight to the National League North without pause in the Conference, for that defeat also sent the club into administration and Conference rules did not allow such clubs membership.

The end of a dream, but, perhaps, the start of another? Departure from the Football League, and the consequences, was indeed very painful. As painful, but longer lasting, as that outrageous kick by Stan Flashman.

Memories of Wembley

Forever etched in my memory will be the day United went to Wembley in the FA Challenge Trophy final. The workload in the build-up to the big day was immense and, although we suffered the disappointment of losing 2-1 to a very good Wealdstone team, it was an unforgettable weekend for the club and town.

We started the Trophy run that season, 1984-85, with a victory at Alvechurch, near Birmingham, on a very foggy day, so foggy, in fact, that it was difficult to follow play.

Regular goalkeeper Kevin Blackwell was unable to play in this game because of injury and well-known local goalie, regularly selected for Lincolnshire, John McPherson stepped into the breach.

In the week running up to this match I travelled with chairman Pat Malkinson, director Alf Bell, player-manager Arthur Mann and player Ray O'Brien to "spy" on the opposition. We received a wonderful welcome from the Alvechurch officials, and we also dropped in on a special evening of entertainment in their Social Club after the match.

Big attraction was two young ladies adept at discarding most of their clothes, something which Messrs Malkinson and Bell seemed to enjoy. (I have photographic evidence to prove this!).

We won the Alvechurch match 2-1 thanks to goals from Bob Lee and Dominic Genovese. It was the first of seven goals for Lee on the run to Wembley. United had a potent strike force in those days with the experience of Lee, and the youthful energy of Chris Cook who notched five goals during the run. And then there was Dominic Genovese, no mean goal-getter himself, who scored in each of the first three games.

The Alvechurch match was the only time we were drawn away in the run-up to the semi-final which was a two-legger against old rivals Altrincham.

The game at York Street against Blyth Spartans brought back memories for older United fans who recalled the occasion of a previous cup clash with the Spartans. This was in the FA Cup in 1954. The first match at Blyth ended in a 1-1 draw, with Ray Wilkins scoring for Boston, but United went out in the replay four days later by the margin of 5-4, Tommy Lowder and Geoff Hazledine scoring two apiece on that occasion.

The Trophy match on the way to Wembley was also a 5-4 thriller, this time with the advantage to Boston with two very late goals from Chris Cook. Bob Lee, Brian Thomson and Dominic Genovese were the other scorers in a great game in which we were 4-2 down with ten minutes to play!

The build-up to this game was full of off-the-field drama, I recall. The original fixture was scheduled for York Street on a Saturday, but it had to be called off on the morning of the game because the pitch was covered in snow and heavy frost. We were enduring a spell of bad weather at the time, so the directors decided to take out an insurance policy to offset the cost of more possible delays and postponements. It was unfit to play on the following Wednesday, Monday and Wednesday again, so that meant four postponements at which point the insurance payment was due.

A thaw set in the following day, and it was all hands on deck in an attempt to get the pitch in a playable condition for that Thursday evening. The hard work paid off and the referee declared that it was fit to play, although there was still water on the pitch.

The result was a thrilling match and the 5-4 win which led to a tie against Wokingham Town when David Gilbert's goal was the only one of the match. This was a highly controversial penalty, and it seemed that the Football Gods were smiling on United.

Old, fierce rivals Runcorn were the next opponents, but goals from Cook, Gilbert and Lee earned us a 3-0 win and eased United into the semi-finals.

We were well-pleased with a 0-0 draw at Altrincham in the first leg, but the second leg at York Street was full of drama before we edged our way into the final with a 3-2 win. It seemed that we were cruising to Wembley when goals from Chris Cook and Bob Lee gave us a 2-0 half time lead, Altrincham then had a man sent off early in the second half, but then they pulled the two goals back in a fighting display typical of their team in those days. The tension became too much for me, I could not watch any more and went for a walk around the car park. There I met club doctor, Dr Taffinder. He could not stand it either. Then, all of a sudden, there was the biggest roar from inside the York Street ground. We both ran back into the ground to discover that Bob Lee had scored what proved to be the winner with only a minute or so remaining, United fans ran onto the pitch, and it took a few minutes to get them off, before they ran back on again to celebrate getting to Wembley!

There was mutual respect between United and Altrincham, and this was highlighted by the magnanimous comment by Altrincham secretary Dave Baldwin who said, after the match: "If we can help Boston United in any way with advice from the experience we have gained from our two visits to Wembley, we shall be only too glad to help. We are obviously disappointed at losing, but it is tremendous for Boston . It is an honour to play at Wembley, and we hope they enjoy it as much as we have done."

For his part, United player-manager, Arthur Mann, showed his admiration for their opponents. "I am full of admiration for Altrincham, and the way they fought back," he said. "They were magnificent . Talk about agony and ecstasy - it was all there."

I can also remember John King their former captain and centre half who had stepped up to be their very successful manager going into the Pilgrims changing room afterwards to congratulate all the lads on their victory, that must have took some doing, but showed what a man he was. Altrincham gained solace the next year when they won the Trophy, beating Runcorn 1-0 in the final, while United fell at the

United players and officials celebrating the second leg semi-final 3-2 win over Altrincham to take the club to Wembley and the F.A. Trophy final in 1985

first hurdle, going out 5-2 away to Kidderminster Harriers, David Gilbert and Peter Denyer scoring for Boston.

The semi-final win was the lift-off to a hectic and exciting build-up to the final. That evening telephone calls were non-stop and all sorts of people wanted to sell us merchandise . From the next day onwards the pace of preparations became even hotter. Pat Malkinson and I were called to a meeting with FA officials at the Holiday Inn at South Mimms, with the FA's Adrian Titcombe leading discussions about arrangements and ticket allocation. That was the signal for even more work. Often from 7am to 10pm, almost every day, in an effort to make sure that Boston United got everything right. My mum even cycled in to bring me hot meals, as I was too busy to leave the club off ice. It was incredible, unbelievably full-on as arrangements had to be made for the sale of tickets and souvenirs, coaches and a train for supporters booked, a coach and meals for players wives, and the staff. It seemed never ending.

**A sea of black and amber met the Boston United team coach
on it's way down Wembley Way to the magnificent national stadium**

When we left York Street on the Friday morning there were a lot of fans there to wave us off, and wish the team well, and there were many more on the route out of Boston. We were booked in to have a look round Wembley Stadium at 4pm on the eve of the match, Wealdstone having been there before us.

The next day was an unbelievable experience, every football man's dream to be at one of the most famous venues in the world of soccer. We sat in the Royal box, and Maureen and Lisa, who had travelled on the wives' coach, sat just behind us. There were about 15,000 United supporters in the 22,000 crowd. It was a special day for them .

Even the result, disappointing though it was to lose 2-1, could not take the shine off the occasion. Wealdstone had clinched the then Gola League championship and were formidable opposition. United had shown disappointing league form and were 17th in the run-up to the final, and a 7-2 trouncing away to Altrincham, who gained their revenge in a small way for defeat in the semi-final didn't help our preparation . Manager Arthur Mann did rest a few of the lads as it was only a week before the final, and we were safe from relegation.

Wealdstone were the better team in the first half went 2-0 up, Kevin Blackwell also saved a penalty but our lads rallied after the interval and, boosted by an early goal

66

from local hero, Chris Cook, we gave them a scare in the second half. Unfortunately David Gilbert had a goal disallowed for offside in the dying moments otherwise it could have been different, but Wealdstone were the best non-league side in the country at that time, even though we had beaten third placed Runcorn and second placed Altrincham in the run up to the final, our opponents and double winners probably deserved their win.

All United fans, and many who were there just for the occasion, will recall the Boston team: Kevin Blackwell, Paul Casey, Ray O'Brien, Ian Ladd, Ged Creane, Mick Laverick, Brian Thompson, Gary Simpson ©, Bob Lee, Chris Cook & David Gilbert; substitute was Gary Mallender who came on in the 78th minute.

Supporters and the town as a whole did their best to lift spirits despite the defeat. Everyone acknowledged the feat in reaching Wembley, and the effort the team had put into the match. The directors had arranged a reception, buffet and entertainment, in the Social Club when the party arrived home that evening, but even then the celebrations were not over.

The Borough Council had arranged for a civic reception in the Assembly Rooms for the next day. There were thousands of people in the Market Place to greet the team who had travelled by open top 'bus from the ground.

United players and staff on the open top bus ride leaving the ground for the journey to the Assembly Rooms ....we were shocked that there were not many people around ....only to be met by thousands in the town centre!

The Mayor at the time was the late Coun Bill North, who gave players and officials a warm welcome, but the star of the show was centre half and club comedian, Mike Czuczman who, although he must have been disappointed in not playing, did not show it as he ran the show from the moment the players appeared on the Assembly Rooms balcony, and kept the laughter ringing out with timely wisecracks during the subsequent meal and speeches.

It was a wonderful weekend for Boston United and the town, with just one downbeat moment... when I discovered that my car had been stolen from the York Street car park on the Saturday evening. When I called the police, I don't suppose that they were too impressed to learn that I had left the keys in the ignition. Fortunately it was discovered later in the car park in the front of the New England. Later, a chastened Bob Lee admitted that he had put it there. It had, he said, seemed like a funny idea at the time. I don't know who felt the bigger fool - him or me!

The good news was that United had received £10,000 as their share of the Wembley gate-compared to the mere £30 from the earlier match at Alvechurch!

Again I have been reliant on the immense amount of research done by the diligent Dr Ken Fox to remind me of subsequent FA Trophy results in my years between starting at York Street and retirement.

1970-71
Selby Town (h) 3-0 (Smith 2, Weaver)
Winterton Rangers (a) 1-0 (Flannagan)
Alfreton (a) 2-0 (Bates 2)
Stockton (h) 2-2 (Bates, McLean), replay 3-1 (Froggatt 2, og),
Wigan Athletic (h) 0-1.

1971-72
Worksop (a) 0-0, replay 2-4 (Froggatt, Svare).

1972-73
Cambridge City (h) 1-0 (Svare),
Bexley United (a) 0-2.

1973-74
Chatham (h) 6-0 (Froggatt 2, Wilkinson 2, Tewley, Conde),
Wigan Athletic (a) 3-2 (Conde 2, Froggatt),
Telford (h) 2-1 (Froggatt, og),
Weymouth (a) 0-3.

1974-75
Buxton (a) 0-0, replay 4-1 (Wilkinson, Fidler, Tewley, Grummett),
Scarborough (h) 1-1 (Howells), replay 0-1.

1975-76
Gainsborough Trinity (h) 0-0, replay 2-4 (Wilkinson, Callery).

1976-77
Wigan Athletic (h) 2-2 (Brown, Bolland), replay 1-2 (Brown).

1977-78
Worcester City (h) 4-1 (Kabia 2, Brown 2), Runcorn (a) 0-1.

1978-79
Atherton (a) 2-1 (Brown, Welch),
Worcester City (h) 4-0 (Kabia 3, Hector),
Stafford Rangers (a) 1-2 (Adamson).

1979-80
Runcorn (a) 1-1 (Adamson), replay 2-1 (Kabia, Hubbard),
Tooting and Mitcham (a) 1-0 (Brown),
Weymouth (h) 2-2 (Poplar 2), replay 1-0 (Poplar),
Dulwich Hamlet (h) 0-0, replay 2-0 (Brown, Poplar),
Mossley (a) semi-final 1-1 (Brown), second leg 1-2 (Brown).

Strongman, defender Steve Thompson missed the second leg because of suspension, and soon afterwards left to join Lincoln City for a £15, 000 fee. These days he can be heard on Radio Lincolnshire as summariser during commentaries on the Imps matches. We were so far behind with our league fixtures by this time that, whatever the result , we had to leave York Street by coach straight after the game to travel all the way to Barrow to fit in another match. Mr Ernest Malkinson and me were the only two club officials to travel with the players. We had an overnight stop at Bolton and you can imagine what a miserable trip it was with everyone so downhearted by that defeat when we were so close to Wembley. The Mossley winner had come just four minutes from time. Neverthless, the lads showed great resilience and we did well at Barrow, winning 1-0, I believe.

1980-81
Gateshead (h) 4-0 (Bartlett 2, Kabia, Callery),
Hitchin Town (h) 0-1.

1981-82
Hyde United (h) 0-1.

69

1982-83
Marine (h) 3-0 (Casey, Cook, Lumby),
Wycombe Wanderers (h) 0-0, replay 1-1 (Garwood),
second replay on neutral ground 2-0 (Garwood, Lumby),
Maidstone United (h) 2-1 (Wood, Gilbert),
Dagenham (a) quarterfinal 1-2 (Garwood).

1983-84
Northwich Victoria (h) 1-1 (Lumby), replay 1-5 (Lumby).

The 1984-85 run which took United to Wembley has already been covered, as has
the following season's quick exit.

1986-87
Frickley Athletic (h) 4-3 (Ward, Cook, Gill, Creane),
Cambridge City (a) 1-0 (Ward),
Barnet (a) 1-1 (Cook), replay 3-3 (Nuttell, Ward 2),
second replay on neutral ground 0-3.

1987-88
Bangor City (a) 2-2 (Cook, Ward), replay 0-0, second replay (h) 2-1 (Wilson 2),
Leyton-Wingate (a) 2-5 (Ward, Wilson).

1988-89
Stafford Rangers (h) 2-0 (Wilson, Ward),
Northwich Victoria (h) 3-2 (Hardy, Hamill, Cook),
Welling United (h) 0-0, replay 0-1.

1989-90
Macclesfield Town (a) 0-0, replay 0-3.

1990-91
Leicester United (h) 3-2 (Cavell 2, McGinley), Runcorn (a) 0-2.

1991-92
Moor Green (a) 3-1 (Howarth, McGinley, Jones),
Macclesfield (a) 0-0, replay 0-2.

1992-93
Spennymoor (a) 2-1 (Jones, Chambers),
Welling United (a) 2-1 (Knight, Munton),
Telford United (a) 1-1 (Jones), replay 4-0 (Jones 3, Stoutt),
Runcorn (h) 0-2.

1993-94- Macclesfield Town (h) 1-1, replay 0-1.

1994-95- Hyde United (a) 0-1.

1995-96- Leek Town (a) 0-0, replay 2-0 (Fee 2),
Chorley (h) 1-1 (Brown) replay 1-2 (Cook).

1996-97
Emley (a) 1-2 (Williams).

1997-98
Belper Town (a) 5-1 (L Chambers, Charles 3, Gowshall),
Hyde United (a) 1-2.

1998-99
Stocksbridge Park Steels (a) 1-1, replay 1-0 (Carmichael).
This first game was postponed on the Saturday and played on the Tuesday. I was aware that we had players unavailable because of suspension if the replay did not take place quickly, so I persuaded Stockbridge to agree to a quick turn around and they came to Boston two days later and, with a full team, we managed to win. This was an example of how a secretary can help the team.
Worksop Town (h) 1-1 (Carmichael), replay 4-0 (Stringfellow, Watts, Hardy, Munton),
Gainsborough Trinity (a) 4-1 (Mason, Stringfellow, Venables, Costello),
Redditch United (h) 2-0 (Venables, Carmichael),
Altrincham (h) 2-0 (Watts),
St Albans City (a) quarter final 1-2 (Watts).

1999-00
Leigh RMI (a) 0-1.

2000-01
Tamworth (a) 3-0 (Norris),
Tiverton (a) 1-2 (Charlery).

2001-02
Northwich Victoria (a) 1-3 (Clare).

2007-08- Gateshead (a) 1-2 (Froggatt).

2008-09
Kidsgrove Athletic (h) 6-0 (Millson, Talbot 2, Ryan, Rowan),
Clitheroe (a) 4-2 (Rowan 2, W Parker, L Parker),

FC United of Manchester (a) 3-1 (Ryan, L Parker 2),
AFC Telford United (h) 1-2 (Rowan).

2009-10
Chorley (h) 3-2 (Davidson 2, Sleath),
Quorn (h) 0-0, replay 2-3 (Newsham, Church).

2010-11
Gainsborough Trinity (h) 2-1 (Newsham, og),
York City (a) 1-0 (Weir-Daley),
Gloucester City (h) 0-1.

2011-12
Workington (h) 1-0 (Newsham),
Hyde (h) 2-1 (Austin, B Fai rclough) ,
Dartford (a) 2-4 (Weir-Daley, Constantine).

2012-13
Colwyn Bay (h) 3-1 (Newsham 2, Sanders),
Skelmersdale United (h) 1-1 (Weir-Daley), replay 1-2 (Newsham).

2013-14
Redditch United (gh) 4-1 (Piergianni, Miller 2, Hall),
Southport (a) 2-1 (Newsham, Piergianni),
Tamworth (a) 0-2.

2014-15
Workington (h) 2-1 (Steer, Southwell),
North Ferriby (a) 1-1 (Newsham), replay 0-2.

FA Cup exploits

I have a mixed bag of FA Cup memories. By my reckoning, United have played in 132 ties during my time in office, and won 67 of them. They have not often had the best of results in this famous old competition, but when they hit the headlines they did it in a big way.

Obviously their two best results have been against Derby County, the 6-1 win at the Baseball Ground in the 1955-56 season still being, I believe, the best away win by a non-League club against a Football League side.

I have recounted how, as a schoolboy, I missed that match, but I did see them bow out of the competition that season with a 4-0 defeat. against star-studded Tottenham Hotspurs, but still earning lots of praise.

I was present as team trainer when, in 1972, United held the Rams to a goalless draw in the mud, again at the Baseball Ground, before losing the replay 6-1. It could, however, so easily have been a sensational victory for The Pilgrims in the first match had it not been for that notorious Derby pitch.

From my large collection of scrapbooks, I can still read what Edwin Buckley wrote in his Sunday Express match report: "Derby manager Dave Mackay should ask his groundsman to dig out the divot of mud which saved his side from humiliating defeat and have it mounted in a glass case in the boardroom Boston United, the side that beat Derby by a staggering 6-1 in one of the FA Cup's most incredible giantkilling acts in 1955, almost pulled off an even more incredible victory. A header from former Leicester City forward, Alan Tewley, was rolling into the net in the 72nd minute when the ball stopped dead, its progress arrested by a big divot of mud on the goal-line ... "

George Rogers of the People wrote: "The performance of Boston, from the Northern Premier League, was a remarkable combination of courage, spirit and unexpected skill."

A young John Blackwell, sporting a trendy hair style and trainer on this epic occasion, figures in photographs of the jubilant United players after the first game. And Andrew, a very young member of the Malkinson dynasty, features as mascot .

The United team which earned so much praise was: Nigel Simpson, John Lakin, Phil Waller, John Moyes, Dick Bate, Billy Howells, Cliff Wright, Alan Tewley, John Froggatt, Jim Conde and Howard Wilkinson. Substitute was Matt Tees.

On Boxing Day, just before the big tie, United had lost at home for the first time in

65 games. One man who was not surprised that United held the mighty Rams to a draw was United secretary Ray Middleton, the man who had played in and, as player-manager, had been the mastermind behind that previous Derby humiliation. He was prepared for a replay. The Derby secretary and directors were taken aback when, in the board room after the first game, he opened his briefcase and produced tickets for the replay. It was not in Ray's nature to do rash things, so he must have given serious thought to this.

I was lucky enough to have a close-up view of United's preparation for this match working under manager Keith Jobling and coach Howard Wilkinson. Before the match Howard had told the Press that he had studied detailed reports of Derby's previous three games. "People may laugh at us for getting reports on a team of Derby's class," he said "but they have enabled us to work on one or two things. Our chances must be 1,000 to one, but you have to be properly prepared to accept that one chance if it comes along."

They had booked the Football Association facilities at Lea Green, on the outskirts of Matlock, from lunch time on Friday. The players trained in the afternoon and then went to a restaurant in Baslow for a steak meal. That would not happen today. The players would be encouraged to eat chicken and pasta, and ordered to have an early night. A strange thing was that no team coach was booked for this big match. We all went in our own cars to Lea Green and, on the morning of the match, drove to the Baseball Ground. I had the kit in my car.

In his team talk there was a strong hint why Howard Wilkinson was to become a successful manager at the highest level. By the time he had finished, the players thought they could win the game.

It was a particularly big day for goalkeeper Nigel Simpson who, only a few weeks earlier, had been playing Boston League football for Kirton School Old Boys after he had been unable to get a first team game while on loan at Holbeach United. Standing in for the experienced and giant-sized Malcolm White, he looked like a schoolboy - although already married - but turned in an absolutely outstanding performance and, in many fans' eyes, was man of the match. It must have been a close thing between Nigel and centre half Dick Bate.

Derby manager, Dave Mackay, not one to give praise easily, put these two on top of the pedestal for their performances in both matches. He then predicted that the Rams would "flatten" United in the replay.

Amateurs Hendon shared the limelight with United that day when they drew at Newcastle United. Unfortunately they lost the replay 4-0.

These matches were played at the height of the miners' strike, and the replay was on Wednesday afternoon as we were not allowed to use floodlights because of the government's plan to restrict the use of electricity. Sadly, the replay saw an end to the United dream as they crashed out of the competition 6-1. This second match came too quickly for the part-t imers.

On the way to that Derby saga, United had beaten Corby Town 2-1 away (Matt Tees 2), Hayes after a replay, being held 0-0 at York Street before winning 2-1 (Tewley, Froggatt) and Hitchin Town 1-0 at home (Conde).

The game at Corby was played in a very hostile atmosphere, with Corby supporters burning the United flag on the terraces. The Hayes replay was in the afternoon because there were no floodlights. It was foggy and the pitch was frozen.

When we played Sheffield United in the 1982-83 season at York Street in the cup we held them to a 1-1 draw courtesy of a goal from Jim Lumby and featured on the BBC's Match of the Day, with Chris Cook featuring as the unusual personality of the round... as he was also the club's groundsman at the time! Manager John Froggatt and players were interviewed and also seen enjoying their pre-match meal, afterwards they were filmed watching the draw for the next round, it would have been a trip to Stoke City in the next round but unfortunately that never materialised because they lost 5-1 in the replay at Bramall Lane. The quick turn-round of the replays in those days gave non-League teams little time to recover from their exertions in the first game.

There was a tailpiece to this replay, however, which nearly robbed United of £5,000 . There was a crowd of 11,000 at Sheffield and, after the game, their secretary, Dick Chester, gave me a note of the gate and receipts. After discussing this with my chairman and directors, we did not think the figures added up correctly and decided to raise a query . Their secretary agreed to look into it and, the next day, he telephoned with an apology. They had forgotten to check one turnstile and there was another £5,000 to come our way.

In the build-up to that Sheffield United match we beat Shifnal Town 4-1 (Cox, Lumby, Cook, Mailender), and Football League side Crewe Alexandra 3-1 (Cook 2, Lumby). Both these matches were at home and Crewe were managed by Peter Morris, who later became manager at York Street. The goal he netted against Shifnal Town was the first FA Cup goal Chris Cook scored for United. It was the first of 21 he scored in the compet ition .

On the only occasion United have been drawn against local rivals, Boston FC (Boston Town now) - in 1970 - the match was given a big build-up by the Boston Standard, including large drawings of the two player-managers, Jim Smith and John Briers, both with receding hairlines, by local artist John Blundy. The two managers had previously been playing colleagues at Halifax. The match ended in a

75

comfortable 4-0 win for United in a game played at Tattershall Ro ad . Brian Bates, Jim Smith (penalty), John Froggatt and John Croy scored the United goals.

Player-manager Smith wrote about this game in his biography where he revealed that the United players were on £20 a man to win plus £20 for every goal difference. He said: "The chairman (Ernest Malkinson) was happy to fork out the cash even if he did confess later that he appealed for offside every time we went forward after we got four."

To reach the tie with Boston FC, United had beaten Holbeach United 4-0 and Lincoln United 1-0, both at home. Player-manager Smith scored in all three games, arguably the most important goal being in the struggle against Lincoln United. Keith Jobling, John Froggatt and Bob Mackay scored the other goals against Holbeach. After the Tattershall Road success, United went on to score a 3-1 win away to Frickley Colliery (Bates 2, Froggatt) to earn another away tie at Southport, then a Football League side.

The Boston Standard organised a train trip for fans to go to this match, and they had a great day out as United gained a stylish 2-0 win thanks to goals from Bates and Mackay. This led to a home tie against another League club, York City - the match that will be remembered for Billy Howells being sent off for an off-the-ball incident spotted by a linesman. Brian Bates scored again for United but they went out of the competition by a 2-1 margin, one of the York goals coming from the penalty conceded by How ells.

The distraught player was banned - by the club - from playing for the first team for four games but, the irrepressible man that he is, he bounced back to regain his status as one of the all-time favourites with the fans. This match was refereed by Roger Kirkpatrick, of Leicester, the man nicknamed Mr Pickwick because of his rotund resemblance of the Dickens character.

In the next season, 1971-72, United were drawn at home to Football League opposition on two occasions, but first they had to win two away games - 3-0 at Winterton Rangers (Hughes, Svare, Wilkinson) and by a similar scoreline at Ellesmere Port (Wilkinson, Svare, Coates). This earned them a York Street tie against Hartlepool United which they won 2-1, thanks to goals from Smith and Froggatt, in front of a crowd of 4,738. In the Hartlepool side that day was the man who has made his name as a much-travelled manager, Neil Warnock .

The next match was also at home against Portsmouth before a crowd of 8,300. I was again the United trainer, but before the game I had been helping my dad to put extra wooden seats in the York Street stand. There was a big contingent of Portsmouth fans and they brought with them the famous Pompey Chimes. We lost by the only goal, scored by the highly rated Mike Trebil cock.

This was a busy day for Boston because, while the match was being played, top pop group T-Rex were rehearsing at the Gliderdrome for their evening performance. That night there was a queue stretching all the way to Boots in the Market Place.

The following season the FA Cup run was only two games. After a 3-1 away win over Bury Town (Conde, Froggatt and Svare), another Jim Conde goal was not enough to save them from a shock home defeat to Lancaster City, by a 2-1 margin.

Alan Tewley, the man who was so close to knocking Derby out of the cup, scored all three goals United netted in the competition in 1974-75, but that was enough to win only one match, 2-1 away to Enderby Town before they were beaten 3-1 away to another League side Chesterfield, John Moyes' old club, for whom striker Ernie Moss was the big threat.

In the next three seasons, United played in only five ties, and suffered the big KO at home three times. In this lean spell, the only win was a commendable 4-3 success away to Kettering when Jim Kabia scored his first FA Cup goal for Boston whose other scorers were Howard Wilkin son , Neil Callery and Gordon Bolland. This earned a home tie against a very confident Lincoln City, under the management of Graham Taylor, but the Imps only scraped home via a Percy Freeman goal.

In 1976-77, United were drawn away to Goole Town, who always seemed to give the Pilgrims a hard t ime. The tie was a 1-1 draw, Dave Adamson - another of United's all-time favourite players - being the scorer, but, having seemingly improved their chances of progress, United lost the replay 3-1, the goal coming from Dave Poplar.

The third game in this lean three-season spell was at home to AP Leamington who created an upset with a 2-1 win (Adamson).

It was during the cup run of 1978-79 that star signing Kevin Hector was introduced to the Boston United team, and he scored two goals in the seven games.

Results that year were:
Heanor (a) won 3-0 (Kabia, Thompson, Brown),
Sutton Town (a) 0-0, replay won 4-0 (Poplar, Moyes, Brown, og),
Retford (a) won 4-1 (Brown, Kabia, Hector, Poplar),
Gainsborough Trinity (h) won 3-0 (Adamson 2, Kabia),
Kettering Town (a) won 3-1 (Hector, Moyes, og),
Tranmere Rovers (a) lost 2-1 (Moyes).

United supporters again travelled by train to this match.

When United visited Ely City in 1979-80 they found themselves playing on an open park with the pitch simply roped off from spectators, and they had a narrow 2-1 win (Kabia and an og). Stamford (a) were beaten 5-0 (Kabia 2, Brown, Adamson, Poplar), and in the next match at Wisbech, United raced into a 5-0 half-time lead (Brown 3, Kabia, Adamson), but crowd trouble during the interval must have upset their rhythm because the final score was 5-1. There were frightening scenes of violence in the ear park after the match.

United bowed out of the competition 2-1 (Brown) in a replay at home to Nuneaton, after drawing 1-1 (Froggatt) at the first attempt.

Although the main stand was only half-built, a crowd of more than 6,000 watched United tumble out of the cup 4-0 against Rotherham in 1980-81 . To reach that stage they had beaten Skegness Town (h) 3-0 (Adamson, Kabia, Simpson), Grantham (a) 3-1 (Leigh, Hubbard, Kabia), Barton Town (h) 2-0 (Hubbard 2), and Corby Town (a) 1-0 (Brown). Jim Kabia's goal was his eighth, and last, in the FA Cup for United.

There was another five-match run the following year:
Sutton Town (h) 2-1 (Phillips, Cox),
Alfreton Town (h) 2-0 (Adamson 2),
North Ferriby (h) 4-0 (Parr, Adamson, Allen, Hubbard),
Dunstable (h) 3-1 (Annable 2, Bartlett), before being beaten 1-0 at home by Kettering.

From 1983-84 there was a run of six seasons with little success. That season we beat Stafford Rangers at home 3-1 (Cook 2, Mailender) but were knocked out 3-0 at home in the next round to League club Bury in a match that saw United's Trevor Parr and Bury's Wayne Entwistle being sent off for fighting, a scrap which continued in the tunnel.

In 1984-85 we lost 3-1 at Barnet (Cook) and, the following year, although we played three matches, we did not survive the first round. All those matches were against Runcorn: (a) 2-2 (Casey, Nuttell), (h replay) 1-1 (Gilbert), (a second replay) 1-4 (Gilbert).

Bogey team Runcorn dashed United's hopes again the following season, after yet another replay. The first match at Runcorn ended in a 1-1 draw (Fee), but Runcorn won the replay 2-1(Lissaman) which took away all the joy we had in beating county rivals Gainsborough Trinity 6-0 at home in the previous round (Hooks, Fee 2, Ward 2, Thomson).

More results in this lean spell were:
1987-88
Welling (h) 1-1 (Wilson), replay 2-3 (Brown, Wilson).

1988-89
Coventry Sporting (h) 8-1 (Beech 2, Creane, Ward, Wilson 4),
Mile Oak Rovers (h) 5-0 (Hamill, Cook4),
Hinckley (h) 3-4 (Cook 2, Wilson).

Things were not much better in 1989-90 for, although United had five matches in the FA Cup, this included two replays:
Leek (h) 3-3 (Moore, Crombie, Hamill), replay 3-0 (Cook, Simpson, Hamill),
Alfreton Town (h) 1-0 (Grocock),
Matlock Town (a) 1-1 (Grocock), replay 0-1.

Chris Cook was in a good run of form when he scored eight goals in an eight-match run which included three replays in 1990-91:
LowestoftTown (h) 7-0 (Cook 4, Cavell 2, Raffell),
VS Rugby (h) 3-1 (Tomlinson 3),
Boreham Wood (a) 1-1 (Cook),
replay 4-0 (Cook 2, Cavell 2),
Dartford (a) 1-1 (Beech), replay 2-1 (Vaughan, Cook),
Wycombe (h) 1-1 (Cavell), replay lost 4-0

A last-minute only goal of the game knocked United out of the FA Cup in 1991-92. This was in a replay at Tamworth, after the clubs had drawn 1-1 (Jones) in the first match at York Street. Jones and Cavell had been on target when Blakenhall, away, had been beaten in an earlier match.

The following season there were two cup matches at York Street. In the first one Kings Lynn were beaten 2-1 (Jones 2) and in the second United lost to Aveley 2-1 (Munton).

There were three matches in 1994-95 and two of them brought victories at home - by 2-0 against Harwich and Parkeston (Munton, Hardwick) and 3-0 over Halstead thanks to a Darren Munton hat-trick. The exit came in a 3-0 defeat away to Heybridge Swifts managed by Gary Hill. Mel Sterland was Boston manager at the time.

Wisbech Town came to York Street and landed a knock-out blow in 1995-96, the margin being 2-1, with Gray being the Boston scorer.

The following season brought the best run for quite a while, the sixth game bringing it to an end. This was at Chester who scored from a penalty after only five minutes, after which United dominated the game but unfortunately The Pilgrims player manager Greg Fee missed a late penalty.

Previous matches had gone as follows:

Maldon (a) 7-2 (Fee, L Chambers, Munton, Mason 3, Williams),

Bishops Stortford (h) 3-0 (Williams, Appleby, L Chambers),

Sudbury Wanderers (h) 10-1 (Williams 3, Hardy, Brown, Appleby 2, Mason, Smaller, Armstrong),

Bedworth United (a) 2-0 (Williams, S Chambers),

Morecambe (h) 3-0 (L Chambers 2, S Chambers).

Uriah Rennie, a prominent top referee of the day, officiated in this match .

Paul Cavell was the only United player to score in the FA Cup in 1997-98, his goal beating Knypersley Victoria (a) 1-0, and another of his efforts not being enough to stop Ilkeston Town, managed by the late Keith Alexander, who won 2-1 on their own ground.

United were odd s-on favourites to beat Congleton in 1998-99, even though the match was away. But they lost 1-0 after player-manager Greg Fee had resigned days earlier with Chris Cook placed in caretaker capacity.

Greg's departure opened the door for the arrival of Steve Evans who, although making a quick impact in league games, did not equal this with immediate cup success.

In 1991-2000 Kingstonian beat United 3-0 in a replay at York Street, after the first match had ended 0-0. Earlier the Pilgrims had beaten Oldbury United (h) 3-1 (Wilson, Norris, Rennie) and Purfleet (h) 4-0 (Stanhope, Rawle 2, Wilson).

Burton Albion, managed by Nigel Clough, held United to a 1-1 draw at Boston in 2000-01 before winning the replay on their own ground 3-2. Ken Charlery scored in both matches and Andrew Stanhope notched the other Boston goal.

There was a shock defeat in United's first round in the following season when they were desperate for the £10,000 prize money. Brigg Town took that with a 1-0 win at York Street, and suddenly all the Boston players became available for sale.

Neil Thompson had taken over as manager from the suspended Steve Evans during the next two seasons, but there was no prize money coming the way of his team eit her. In 2002-03 they travelled to Northampton Town to put up a good fight before going down 3-2 (Battersby, Higgins) and the following year, in another away game, they were beaten 3-0 by Macclesfield Town.

Steve Evans was back in charge for 2004-05 when results were:

80

Hornchurch (h) 5-2 (L Thompson, McManus 2, Noble, Ellender),
Hereford United (a) 3-2 (Lee, Kirk 2),
Hartlepool United (a) 0-0, replay 0-1.
Hartlepool missed a penalty in injurytime in the first match.

In the next season United made an impressive start in their bid for cup glory:
Buxton (h) 4-1 (Leabon 2, Galbraith, Froggatt)
Hinckley United (h) 4-1 (Leabon 2, Crane, Thompson)
before making the long trip to Workington only to be beaten 1-0 thanks to a controversial penalty... only referee Brian Saunders could tell you why he awarded it!

In 2008-09 results were:
Glapwell (h) 6-0 (Melton, Leabon, Ryan 3, Rowan),
Stamford AFC (a) 2-1 (Froggatt 2),
Southport (a) 2-0 (Leabon, Rowan),
Cambridge (h) 2-3 (Leabon, Ryan).

From then onwards it was disappointment all the way towards my retirement.
2009-10
Loughborough Dynamoes (h) 4-2 (Newsham, Suarez, Pearson 2),
Lowestoft (h) 0-1.

2010-11
Worcester City (h) 2-3 (Newsham, Yates).

2011-12
Kidsgrove Athletic (h) 0-0,
replay 0-2.

2012-13
Kettering Town (h) 1-0 (B Fairclough),
Tadcaster Albion (a) 2-0 (Jones, Newsham) - two days before this match the pitch was badly flooded ...in fact the water level was over a foot high in the changing rooms and social club... so you could imagine whatthe pitch was like!
Altrincham (h) 1-3 (Jones).

2013-14
Stafford Rangers (a) 4-0 (Weir Daley 2 Miller 2),
Brackley Town (a) 0-2 .

2014-15
Dereham Town (h) 3-1 (Fallah, Southwell, Mills),

Leek Town (a) 0-2 .

With results as disappointing as these in the final years of my working life with United, I was so glad to have experienced the excitement of those early years!

Chasing players

Good footballers, at whatever level, are always in demand. And they know it.

Boston is not in the best position geographically to be an attraction to many of the best but, over the years, the United have been able to field some from the top echelons of the game, including some internationals.

Perhaps the best they ever tempted to the town was way back in 1936, long before I was born, when Freddie Tunstall signed. He was a star left winger with Sheffield United, and scored the only goal when they beat Cardiff City 1-0 in the FA Cup final at Wembley in 1926 . Moreover, he played for England seven times, and captained them twice.

Freddie was United manager on four different occasions (1937-39, 1945-47, 1952-53 and 1964-65) and became well-known in the town as he stayed to live the rest of his life in Boston.

Another top signing, of course, was England B international Ray Middleton, whose time as player-manager brought unprecedented success to Shodfriars Lane, before it was named York Street.

Common factor in these signings was long-time club benefactor, Ernest Malkinson. As the years rolled by, he was no less tenacious in pursuit of men he wanted for his team. He brought big, brawny ex-West Bromwich forward Derek Kevan to York Street in the days of Don Donovan as player-manager.

I suppose it was not too difficult to persuade the elegant Gordon Bolland back to his home town when a dodgy knee ended his Division One career. After all he was a product of the old Burgess Pit "academy" and was happy to settle once again in his home town.

It was a different matter, however, with Kevin Hector, the England international striker, when he had finished a stint in Canada with Vancouver Whitecaps. Anyone who knew Mr Malkinson well soon realised that he had a close friendship with food, and the fact that he was willing to forego his Sunday lunch to go in pursuit of Hector showed how keen he was to capture a man who still had a lot of good football left in him. That is just what the then chairman did.

United were away to Workington on the Saturday, stopping overnight on Friday in Keswick. Brian Bates was supposed to be in charge of the team but he never turned up because, I believe, of some problem over the signing and playing of Hector. After the Workington game, Mr Malkinson asked me to go with him the next day to try to complete the signing of the ex-Derby man who had played for the Rams in that memorable FA Cup tie when United had held them to a goalless draw at the old Baseball Groun d. Despite the fact that the chairman, and his wife, had driven the long haul back from Workington, he was ready early on Sunday morning to start the Hector hunt.

He lived in Allestree, near Derby, and we knocked on doors until we found his home. Mr Malkinson announced that we had come to sign him for Boston United, and we would not be leaving until we had his signature on the appropriate forms. We were invited in and negotiations - mainly financial - took a long time, pretty well all afternoon in fact before he eventually signed, by which time the chairman was acutely aware that he had not had his Sunday lunch!

On the way home we searched desperately for somewhere that might be open and serving food, but it was not until we reached Sedgebrook Transport Cafe that we found somewhere, and even then we had to plead for some food before we were served. We made our way back to Boston triumphant that we had got our man, and our (very late) Sunday lunch.

Kevin Hector was a highly rated player. He went on to return to Derby County and was still capable of holding his own in the old Division One... now The Premiership of course.

Another England international to sign for Boston United was Leeds United's marauding right back, Mel Sterland, who became player-manager. He had played a key role in ex-United manager Howard Wilkin son 's success in steering Leeds to the Division One championship.

I have two stories which stick in my mind to tell about Mel. One Tuesday tea time, when we were scheduled to train at Newark later that evening, I received a surprise telephone call from former United player, Gordon Simmonite. After finishing his playing career, Gordon, a popular defender at York Street and at Lincoln City, had joined the Police Force and, at the time of the call, he was a sergeant stationed in Sh effi eld. His news was that Mel Sterland was in custody and would not be able to take training that night!

Mel lived in Dore, near Sheffield, and a stolen safe, said to be containing £63,000 in cash and postal orders etc, had been found in his garage . The safe had been taken from Dore Post Office during a break-in the previous evening. Mel, of course, did not know anything about it and was eventually released without charge when it transpired that someone who had been involved in the raid, had dumped the safe in the garage without Mel's knowledge.

The second story involves a testimonial match. In recognition of his service to Leeds

United, Mel had already had one testimonial match, but had been promised a second one. Leeds, however, were unable to stage it at Elland Road, and we were asked to host it at York Street. Howard Wilkinson brought a strong team to play a Boston United XI, and included in it were players like Mark Bright and Scottish international, and subsequently Scotland manager, Gordon Strachan.

Everything went well. It was a great game, watched by a crowd of around 3,500, there was a buffet and reception in the Social Club afterwards, and everyone went home happy. Or so we thought. Later that evening, however, I received a telephone call from Mel who was unhappy. He felt that we had not announced the correct att endance. He thought that there were more people present than we had said . I was fuming at the suggestion, and drove straight to the Gliderdrome to see chairman Pat M alk inson, who was equally angry at the accusation, and instructed Mel to report to the ground the following day, accompanied by his wife, to sort things out .

Clarrie Atterby, a highly respected Borough Councillor and former Mayor of Boston, was in charge of the turnstiles at the time, and he was also asked to attend. Together we went to each turnstile and checked the figures against the money taken and, to Mr and Mrs Sterland's embarrassment, everything turned out to be correct. After a few strong words, the chairman gave them the money exactly as it had been taken, all in small change and in carrier bags . Later, we received an apology.

Signing top player Mick Marsh was seen as a coup by Steve Evans at the time. I remember it because it caused me a lot of unnecessary hassle. In his wisdom, Mr Evans did not want the completion of formalities done by fax or post. He insisted that I went all the way to Southport to complete the signing - although Mike Marsh was not going to be there, having already signed the form and gone back home to Ormskirk.

All I needed was the signature of Southport secretary, Ken Hilton, all of which could have been done by fax. Steve, however did not like this idea. So I made the four hour journey to Southport to meet Ken Hilton at their Haigh Avenue Gro und . Completion of the form took all of five minutes and, after a brief chat with Ken, a good friend of mine, and a drive along the sea front, I made my way back to Boston in dreadful conditions, and without food until I arrived home.

The Southport secretary could not believe that I had been ordered to drive all that way for one signature when it could all have been done by fax, or post!

Working with managers

During my time at Boston United I have worked with 26 managers. For most of that time it was a privilege, no more so than with the very first.

Jim Smith. From his humble start at York Street in 1969 Jim went on to big things but never became too grand to keep in touch.

He was the man who invited me to join the club after he had been released by Lincoln City. He had been spotted by Ernest Malkinson as a good choice for player-manager at Boston, and proved to be a canny choice as he brought new professionalism to the club and laid foundations that brought continued success long after he had started his climb in the Football League managerial ranks.

As a player, he was a good, old-fashioned midfielder who popped up with a surprising number of goals in key matches. Ambitious and hard-working it was obvious from those early days that he was likely to make the grade and the point was proved as he moved to Colchester United, Blackburn Rovers, Birmingham City, Newcastle United, Derby County, Queen's Park Rangers and Oxford United, and as assistant to Harry Redknapp at Portsmouth, earning the nickname of the Bald Eagle over the years as his hair became even thinner than it was in his playing days.

Jim never forgot his roots, and the part Boston played in giving him the chance to learn his trade in football management, and was subsequently always happy to bring his teams down to play at York Street.

I was only too glad to help him bring both Derby County and Newcastle United to the area for training and team-building breaks, which included matches in Boston. Alongside him at Derby was former England manager Steve Mcclaren, ironically, as I write, back in his second spell as manager of the Rams.

One year, when bad weather was seriously hampering football, I arranged for his Birmingham City to play a practice match against Norwich City at York Street.

Jim liked a night out which Maureen and I often shared with him and his wife Yvonne, after a Saturday match. His favourite drink was a pint of beer or a glass of red wine. When he brought Derby County to the area, he invited us to a night out at the Cowbridge Inn along with his staff.

Now living in Spain, and always complaining that it is too hot, he still keeps in touch and, on the night of my surprise retirement party, he telephoned to apologise for not being able to attend.

Keith Jobling (1972-1975}

When Jim Smith left for Colchester in October 1972, he recommended that Howard Wilkinson should take over his role, but the astute Mr Malkinson thought he was too young, and he appointed Keith Jobling instead, but asked Howard to assist as player-coach. Together, of course, they plotted that famous 0-0 FA Cup draw away to Derby County.

Keith was a one-club man before he joined United as one of Jim's first signings. He had joined Grimsby as a teenager in 1953, and played 450 League games for them as a central defender. He turned out to be a good, solid signing for United, playing until the age of 39.

When he took over, United were 40 games into a long unbeaten run and, under the Jobling management, they went on to take that run to 51 games. The Jobling-Wilkinson partnership went on to complete the work Smith had started by clinching the Northern Premier League championship with a 4-1 win at home to Altrincham. A key result in that achievement had been a 0-0 draw away to Wigan Athletic on the previous Monday.

Many fans - and I can count myself as one of them - still drool over the end-of-season performances that earned them the non-League Champions of Champions title in matches against Southern League champions, high-profile Kettering Town. Jim Conde was top scorer with 26 goals that season.

The next season their mouthwatering cup run resulted in a build-up of fixtures, after, early in the campaign, they had found it difficult to earn points away from home. They recovered well from the exertions of their cup run, however, and made up lost ground with an unbeaten run that took in February, March and April, and also included victory in the NPL Cup final, 2-1 over old rivals Altrincham. With the end of season fast approaching, Wigan had eased into top spot but victory in their last match against Morecambe would still give United the title. This they achieved by a 2-0 margin thanks to goals by Conde and Alan Tewley.

In the close season, United lost strikers Conde (£2,000 to Kettering Town}, John Froggatt, who joined Jim Smith and Bobby Svare at Colchester, in a £6,000 move, and Matt Tees, who retired at the age of 33, and the next season saw them drop to 12th place in the league - a dramatic drop from previous recent standards. Keith, an amiable and likeable man, stepped down as manager in the light of these results and exit from the FA Trophy.

Howard Wilkinson (1975-1977}

Scotland manager Gordon Strachan was quoted in the Daily Mail as saying this about the former Boston United player-coach and manager: "I loved him . This guy was honest, professional, drove people to the limit. Everybody who ever bumped into him will be thankful they did."

I agree completely with these sentiments. Howard did a great job at Boston, was a top tactician and left no stone unturned in his preparation for matches. His contribution to that famous 0-0 draw at Derby was testament to his managerial potential which blossomed as he moved on to NPL rivals, Mossley, Notts County, Leeds United, Sheffield Wednesday and, for a short spell, Sunderland. He also had a short-term contract with Chinese champions, Shanghai Shenhua.

It was his record at Leeds that put him among the elite. He joined the club when they were third from bottom of the Second Division, in 1988, and took them to the old First Division title in 1992 when he won the Manager of the Year award, and became the last English manager, to this day, to have coached the team to win the major title in English football.

It was when he was a member of this championship-winning team that Gordon Strachan became so well acquainted with him- as did an impending United player-manager Mel Sterland.

Jim Smith brought Howard to Boston as player-coach from Brighton and Hove Albion and, previously, Sheffield Wednesday. While playing at Boston, he trained to be a teacher, but the classroom did not detain him long before he went into full-time football management.

He was subsequently appointed the Football Association's Technical Director when he played a major role in the development of FA facilities at Burton, and, for two games, was caretaker manager of England when Glen Hoddle departed. He had also been manager of England's semi-professional side.

Howard is still a prominent figure in football, being chairman of the League Managers' Association and is their representative on the Football Association who selected him on to the panel which interviewed Gareth Southgate for the England manager's job.

Among his varied football activities, he was also chairman of Sheffield Wednesday for a short time while they were seeking new owners.

He still keeps in touch, with a Christmas card each year, and called for a chat on my retirement.

I would rate Howard as United's best ever manager and, perhaps unfortunately for the long line of successors, they have all suffered by comparison to him and Jim

Smith in the eyes of myself and, I am sure, many long-standing supp orters.

Freddie Taylor and Gordon Bolland (1977)

When Howard Wilkinson moved on, chairman Ernest Malkinson was in no hurry to appoint a permanent replacement and asked senior players Gordon Bolland and Freddie Taylor to see the season out, and I was able to help them in the administration side of t hing s. Boston-born Gordon had returned to the town after a wonderful career at the top level with Chelsea, whom he joined as a schoolboy, Norwich City and Millwall.

Gordon Bolland and myself modelling the latest kit bags supplied to the players by local business Morley Sports

His class was still apparent at York Street, but his dodgy knees meant that he struggled at times in the hurly-burly of semi-professional football. When he retired from the game he became a tyre salesman with local company Fossitt and Thorne, and latterly has been a taxi driver in Boston.

Freddie Taylor came to Boston from Gainsborough Trinity as a winger, but was converted into a full-back by Howard Wilkin son. This proved to be a master stroke as he became a key member of the team. Both men were popular with the players who responded well to clinch the Northern Premier League title.

Mick Walker (1977-1978)

Mick Walker, a friend of Howard Wilkinson, was a well-respected coach in football circles and came to Boston after a spell coaching the Singapore team, bucking the trend of chairman Ernest Malkinson for having a player-manager, his version of BOGOF {Buy One Get One Free - in other words get a manager and good player for one wage).

An intelligent, articulate man, he left the club after a disagreement with the chairman over the manner in which Kevin Hector was brought to Boston. Subsequently he went on to manage Notts County and had coaching duties with other Football League clubs, including Leeds United, but it is hardly likely that he will come first to mind when fans recall men who made a lasting impact at York

St reet.

Albert Phelan (1980-81}

It was back to the player-manager preference when Albert Phelan was appointed .
He was a popular promotion from the playing ranks, and I can only say that in my
opinion the Sheffield-born defender was a smashing fellow, someone I got on with
really well.
From 1977 to his departure in 1981, he made 110 appearances for United and, as
manager, took us to fourth place in the league and to the FA Trophy semi-finals. He
had a long, successful, career with Chesterfield, and moved to Halifax before
arriving at Boston. He also coached youngsters at Sheffield Wednesday.

John Froggatt (1981-1983}

A man I regard as one of United's all-time greats, John Froggatt, succeeded Albert
Phelan as manager to continue the trend of having thoroughly good, decent
individuals in charge of team affairs.

I got on really well with John, and he still keeps in touch . When Jim Smith signed
him from Buxton for a mere £500, it must have been the best deal he ever
negotiated, certainly his acquisition must have been United's biggest bargain. John
had been with Notts County before stepping down to Buxton, but his career was
revived at York Street and under Jim Smith's management.

He linked up with his old strike partner Bobby Svare (what a partnership they were)
to play under Jim again at Colchester in a deal that brought £6,000 into United
coffers, and later moved to Port Vale and Nort hampton , each time for £10,000,
before arriving back in Boston in 1980.

During his two spells at Boston he played something like 200 games, and was a
regular goal-getter. He also proved to be a good manager before returning to his
fall-back career as a painter and decorator after a section of supporters turned
against their one-time favourite following a decline in results.

Arthur Mann (1983-1985)

Another popular manager was Arthur Mann, someone I enjoyed working with and
a fitting man to take the club to Wembley to the FA Trophy final. Unfortunately, the
fortunes of football managers being as they are, he was relieved of his duties, after
a spell of disappointing results, six months after that big day out .

Arthur had a lovely family, wife Sandra and three children, including son Neil who
played for Grimsby Town and Hull City, and they were devastated when he died,

90

aged 51, in an industrial accident in a scrap yard where he was working after no longer being involved in football. I was among a good contingent from United who attended his funeral when a Scottish piper led us all into church.

He had been born in Falkirk and started his soccer career with Heart of Midlothian, where he attracted the attention of Manchester City when they were managed by Joe Mercer and Malcolm Alli son. City paid £65, 000 for his services, a substantial sum in 1969.

A fear of flying proved a big obstacle to him becoming a first team regular with City who were involved in European competitions, but other clubs were keen to sign him for sizeable fees - Blackpool, Notts County, where he made more than 240 appearances over seven years, Shrewsbury Town and Mansfield Town.

In his first season at Boston United he missed only one game and was voted Player of the Year. He left Boston briefly, to join his former Notts County colleague, Don Masson, at Kettering Town, but when he returned he took over from John Froggatt as manager but the team finished a disappointing 17th in the Alliance Premier League.

Early next season he broke his leg in two places in a Lines Senior Cup match against Grantham, but returned to play again and, when he left Boston, he went on to play for Telford before becoming assistant to Alan Buckley who managed at Grimsby and West Bromwich Albion.

Ray O'Brien (1986-1987)

Next man in the managerial hotseat at York Street was Arthur Mann's assistant, Ray O'Brien, the Dublin-born defender who won several international caps for Eire and, over 10 years, had more than 300 Football League appearances for Notts County . He had joined County from Manchester United for a fee of £45,000.

Another nice guy, with a lovely family, Ray was brother-in-law to Eire international Nigel Worthington who later became manager of his country, and of Sheffield Wednesday and Norwich City.

After leaving full-time football he went into the printing industry, but, after leaving United, he stayed in the game, first as manager of Corby Town and than general manager of Arnold Town. A bad spell of results, including exit from the FA Cup, led to Ray's departure from United.

George Kerr (1987-1989)

Searching desperately for success, United decided to put things in the hands of an experienced Football League manager, and George Kerr was the man selected. As a player he had a lot of Football League experience with Barnsley, Bury, Oxford and Scunthorpe United and, as a manager, he was twice at Lincoln and guided Grimsby Town to the Division Three title. He could not save Rotherham from relegation when he was manager there, and Lincoln were relegated into Division Four while he was in charge. He was sacked by the Imps just before they dropped into the Confe rence.

With Ronnie Reid as his assistant, he took United to third place in the Conference in his second year after being given cash to sign players like Paul Shirtliff, from Frickley, and Martin Hardy, from Worksop . Ironically, he also brought his eventual successor, Dave Cusack, to the club. The changeover came when United were in danger of relegation.

George brought a lot to the club, was very experienced and knew the game inside out. He worked part-time at Boston, continuing to live in Grimsby. One memory I have of him is the occasion when the directors instructed me to buy bottles of whisky for each of the players as a Christmas gift . I distributed them on the coach after an away game and, by the time we arrived back at Boston, George's bottle was empty!

Dave Cusack (1990-1992)

Dave Cusack and myself receiving the keys to our new club cars from Sandicliffe Ford

Dave Cusack was an outstanding central defender for the Pilgrims, having had a lot of League experience with Sheffield Wednesday, Southend United, Millwall and Doncaster Rovers where he was appointed player-manager. With the help of re-instated Ronnie Reid as his assistant, he halted the decline at York Street, steered the team away from the threat of relegation, and then took them to eighth in the Conference in the next season. Unhappy with the playing budget for the following season, he departed for Kettering into a job which lasted only two months.

A popular figure at Boston, Dave worked as a car salesman for Ford dealers Sandicliffe while working for United, and had the misfortune to lose two cars which went up in flames.

Wherever United travelled, Dave was followed by an attractive young lady who appeared to be his biggest fan.

He was the go-to man if you wanted anything, and got me my first mobile phone when the league decreed that clubs must carry a phone on the coach when travelling to matches. He appeared to have contacts who could get anything you wanted! He was always good fun, and easy to work with. My girls became good friends with his children, Tom and Lucy. He also went on to manage Dagenham and Redbridge who later became fierce rivals to United.

Peter Morris {1992-1994)

While Dave Cusack was moving over to Kettering Town, Peter Morris was making the journey in the opposite direction to become his successor as manager of Boston United where he took his seventh full-time managerial appointment.

I shared an office with him, and saw at first hand how professional he was. He was a quiet, serious man who brought a lot of new players to the club, and introduced his friend John Drewnicki who became a director of the club.

Peter Morris and myself welcoming new signing Drew Coverdale to Boston United. Drew and Paul Bastock shared a club house in Spain Place

He had been manager of Crewe Alexandra when United beat them in the FA Cup in the 1982-83 season . Other clubs he managed were Mansfield Town, Peterborough United, Southend United, Nuneaton Town, Kettering Town (twice) and Kings Lynn (also twice).

In his playing days he was a highly rated wing half, starting as a youth with Mansfield Town where, in two spells, he played 328 first team games. He was also a consistent regular with Ipswich Town (220 games) and Norwich City (66 games).

Mel   Sterland (1994-1996)

Mel Sterland was a player who had tasted life at the very top of the game before becoming United's player-manager in 1994.

As a full-back he had played 279 games for Sheffield Wednesday, nine for Glasgow Rangers and 114 for Leeds United under the management of Howard Wilkinson where he was able to celebrate a Division One championship win. He was also an under 21, and 'B' international before gaining one full England cap.

An ankle injury had prompted his retirement from elite football, but he managed to play 29 games for United before moving on to play for Denaby whom he helped to win the Northern Counties East League.

He was also manager of Stalybridge Celtic when they were relegated from the Conference, and later played for Hallam .

A likeable and popular figure, I am reliably informed that he was banned from speaking to the Boston Target newspaper after they had published something which did not meet with thechairman's approval. Mel ignored the ban, I am told.

Greg Fee (1996-1998)

Greg Fee played 300 first team games in two spells with Boston United. He was signed from Kettering Town in September 1986 and stayed one season before being transferred to Sheffield Wednesday for £20,000, and he made 26 first team appearances in four seasons.

He had loan spells with Preston North End, Northampton and Orient before moving to Mansfield Town in 1990-91. He made 60 appearances for the Stags before re-joining Boston United in 1993-94, and then became player-manager with Chris Cook as his assistant at the start of the 1996-97 season and stayed in charge until he resigned in September 1998, when he moved to Telford as a player. He subsequently played for Emley and was also player-manager at Gainsborough Trinity .

He has attempted to return as manager several times when the post has become vacant at York Street but I don't think he has ever been seriously considered, because he has been out of the management game for so long, but kept his eye in as a coach and a scout for various top clubs.

A lovely guy, Greg was always popular with players, supporters and staff.

Steve Evans (1998-2002 and 2004-2007)

Following the resignation of Greg Fee as player-manager and a few games in caretaker charge of Chris Co ok, a 1-0 defeat in the FA Cup at lower league Congleton ushered in the whirlwind that was Steve Evans, controversial and successful.

United's initial meteoric rise under his command had ecstatic fans believing that he could walk on water; little did they realise that he would end his reign treading through the sticky stuff.

While results were outstanding on the pitch, many ignored his expletive-laden rants at match day officials, and the opposition bench, or excused it as " passion" . The more discerning thought it was just boorish behaviour that tarnished the reputation of the club.

At the start, however, it was like a breath of fresh air hitting York Street. He started at full pelt and, within days, I went with him to watch a match at Alfreton Town. United became a revolving door for players, in and out, and he startled us all by the contacts he had, and with his persuasive powers in attracting good players to the club.

Steve arrived at Boston having managed village side Gedney Dyke, Holbeach United and, very successfully, Stamford AFC. Along the way there was also a short spell at Corby Tow n.

For a start he was part-time at York Street, combining his football work with a job as salesman for a company in Long Sutton . He told us that previously he had been a much-travelled salesman for Budweiser, a post that entailed trips to the USA. He told us stories of how he had been in the company of many famous people. Pamela Anderson and Alan Shearer were two I recall being mentioned .

He lived near the East of England Showground in Peterborough, and brought his brother Gerard with him to Boston to act as coach and scout, and take in many other tasks. In his first season he transformed United from relegation candidates to runners-up in the Dr Martens League, a remarkable achievement.

It was all looking too good to be true as he steered the team to promotion to the Conference in the following season. Now a full-time club, it was not long before, under his rumbustious charge, the dream of Football League status was realised.

Unfortunately he did not enjoy the fruits of his labour because, as an investigation in club affairs was launched by the Football Association, he was suspended by the club's new owners, and he resigned when charges were brought against him by the FA. Subsequently he was banned from football for 20 months and fined £8,000 by the FA.

He was re-appointed as manager in February 2004, under the new regime led by Jon Sotnick, and enjoyed a taste of Football League management until United were relegated in 2007, after which he left to become manager of Crawley Town, again overseeing success on the field of play.

Subsequently he moved up to the Championship with Rotherham United and Leeds United before moving down the leagues again to manage Division Two Mansfield Town.

Steve Evans' stay at Boston brought some of my most exciting times in football, but also was the forerunner to the most worrying and depressing days as the methods he employed in chasing success, and in my opinion, brought the club to its knees and near extinction. I felt that he was a bully to me, and to other people at the club.

Neil Thompson (2002-2004)

Neil Thompson was the man who kept the managerial seat warm while Steve Evans served his suspension. He was, in fact, one of Evans' inspired signings, joining United from Scarborough to help with coaching, particularly of the defence, and was drafted into the team on occasions, playing nine times for the first team.

Neil was a real football man, knowledgeable and popular. A good guy to work alongside. He had a wealth of experience as a reliable defender with Nottingham Forest, Ipswich, Barnsley, Oldham, York City and Scarborough. He also managed the latter two clubs.
After leaving Boston, he went to work with the development squad at Leeds United.

Tommy Taylor (2007-2008)

The first managerial appointment of the David Newton-Neil Kempster regime was Tommy Taylor who had been Chief Scout at Peterborough United and, as a player, had appeared 230 times for Orient and 340 times for West Ham where he won the

FA Cup in the 1975 2-0 victory over Fulham.

He was a very knowledgeable football man, with lots of contacts, and well liked by everyone. His son, Lee, was physiotherapist with United under Steve Evans.

After the rollercoaster years of the volatile Scotsman, the new owners were keen to make a different kind of appointment. The position was advertised, and interviews took place at Chestnut Homes' headquarters in

Tommy Taylor presenting me with a signed shirt for my 60th birthday

Langworth. Messrs Newton and Kempster, Chris Cook, Craig Singleton and myself were the interviewing panel.

Applicants interviewed included Ian Atkins, John McDermott, Graham Barrow, Brendan Phillips, Steve Welsh and Morrell Mason.

The interviews lasted until about 8pm and, eventually, it was decided to offer the position to Ian At kins. I understand that he turned down the opportunity to manage Boston United and, coincidentally, a late application came in the next morning. It was from Tommy Taylor. An interview was arranged quickly, and his appointment was announced later that day.

Tommy and his wife, Pat, moved from their home near Kettering to live on London Road, Boston. They were a popular couple, and I think they enjoyed their short time in Boston. Tommy brought a lot of experience to the job , having worked overseas, and been assistant manager at Maidstone United, followed by spells as manager at Cambridge, Orient, Darlington and Farn borough.

He left Boston in 2008 and subsequently managed Kings Lynn and worked again overseas, in Finland and Norway.

Steve Welsh (2008-2009)

Steve Welsh was known as Captain Chaos at the club, and work colleagues often wondered if his wardrobe contained any trousers because he always wore shorts, whatever the weather.

He was given the job after being caretaker for a month following Tommy Taylor's departure. He was one of the nicest people I have ever worked with at Boston

United, and someone who really loved the game of football.

As a player, he was a central defender who made one appearance for Cambridge United before becoming a first team regular, and captain, at Peterborough United. After a loan spell at Preston, he moved to Scotland and had spells with Partick Thistle, Dunfermline Athletic and Ayr United.

When released by Ayr in 1999, he joined Lincoln City . He also played for Kings Lynn while working as Football in the Community Officer at Sincil Bank.

He was manager at Spalding United before joining Boston United as youth team coach, and then took charge of the Centre of Excellence after Neil Richardson left.

As manager at Boston he achieved just 11 wins from 34 games, and his contract was not renewed. He went on to be in charge of youth at Ilkeston, where he was also first team assistant manager.

Paul Hurst and Rob Scott (2009-2011}

Paul Hurst and Rob Scott came in, as joint managers, from Ilkeston where they had shown great potential. It was a first-class appointment.

They introduced new ideas into the club and were professional in everything they did, as well as being strong disciplina   rians. They brought in good players who took us to the NPL play-off final away to Bradford Park Avenue, a match we won in the dying minutes to gain promotion to the Conference Nort h.

Under their management United appeared to be going places but, unfortunately for us, they were tempted away by Grimsby Town where, again, they were successful.

The partnership was broken when Rob left the Mariners after a dispute involving a player, but Paul continued to take the club back in to the Football League.

I really enjoyed working with both of them. They could be said to be a Good Cop-Bad Cop partnership. They were two completely different characters. Rob was the "hard" man, sometimes volatile, and Paul was the quiet thinker.

It was something of a surprise in football circles when, in October 2016, Paul left the Mariners to try to save struggling Shrewsbury Town from relegation from Division One. He has really turned them around and was rewarded with a move to Championship club Ipswich Town. Unfortunately he didn't last long and is now looking for another job, which I don't think will take too long.

Jason Lee and Lee Canoville (2012)

When Paul Hurst and Rob Scott left for Grimsby, senior players Jason Lee and Lee Canoville were put in charge of team affairs at Boston. Striker Jason had bags of experience in League football, and Lee was one of the most respected players at the club. Again they were good people to work with; Lee continued to play but Jason was mainly in the dugout.

When playing with Nottingham Forest and Charlton Athletic, Jason was famous for his "pineapple" hairstyle, always an attraction for matchday photographers.

Jason went on to work for the Professional Footballers' Association and Lee runs his own coaching business around the Nottingham area.

Graham Drury (2012-2013)

When Jason and Lee left the club, the manager's position was advertised once again and, in my opinion, the Board made one of their biggest mistakes in appointing another former Stamford manager as the team boss. Even though he was a really nice guy, Graham did not seem able to cope with the demands of Conference North football, bringing in too many players from lower leagues, and who were not of the required standard.

He brought in a new coach, Paul Holden, who did most of the work on the training pitch while Graham watched from the touchline. Later he also sought the help of ex-Pilgrim and former Lincoln City player, Dean West, at training sessions.

Results were poor and the owners decided to let Graham leave after only a few months, although he has since had some success as manager again at Stamford, especially in taking them on an impressive FA Cup run in 2016.

Dennis Greene (2013-2016)

The successor to Graham Drury was Essex Boy, Dennis Greene who had been an unsuccessful interviewee when Graham was appointed. Regarded by some as a bit of a "Jack the Lad" who was familiar with the local night scene, Dennis had been manager of St Neots when they were promoted from the United Counties League to the Southern Premier League.

He had a wealth of experience as a player, being in the Conference-winning team at Wycombe in 1992-93 when they also won the FA Trophy under the leadership of Martin O'Neill. His other clubs included Dagenham and Redbridge, Harlow, Bishop Stortford, Stansted, Epping, Stambridge, and Chelmsford City.

He had a lot of contacts in the game and took United to two unsuccessful play-offs, against Chorley and North Ferriby United.

I got on really well with Dennis, and enjoyed working with him even though his liking for loan signings, often late on a Friday, sent the stress levels soaring as I endeavoured to get the players registered in time to play the following day.

He signed, and developed, some good players for United, but five or six key players left the club in the summer of 2016 and

Dennis Greene signing three quality players in Spencer Wier-Daley, Ian Ross and Marc Newsham

replacements were not of the same quality. He appeared to lose focus and disappointing results led to his departure.

Dennis, I recall, set me a poser early in my retirement when he telephoned to see if it would be OK if his partner, Carla George, the Radio Lincolnshire journalist, could take to a match the dog he had recently purchased for her. Luckily, I was able to pass the request on to the Safety Officer, but I do recall being licked to death by the same dog at an away match!

One man who has been involved with a number of managers at York Street, either as coach or assistant manager, is Ronnie Reid who was a good non-League player, and a brilliant coach .

He, of course, played for United as well as for a number of other clubs. He was a difficult-to-handle old fashioned centre forward and I remember in one match, when he was playing for Worksop Town, he ran the United defence ragged.

Ronnie was well respected in the game and took over as manager at Stafford Rangers. He was also manager of the England semi-professional team, and went on to run the academy at Sheffield United with great success, winning the FA Youth Cup.

In my opinion he was one of the best coaches in non-League football, and certainly one of the best to serve Boston United.

Another top-quality player who helped with coaching was the much-travelled £1 million Premier League Neil Redfearn, a brilliant footballer and free kick expert, and someone I really liked.

He went on to earn a great deal of praise for the manner in which he ran the Leeds United Academy, and took over as first team manager on a couple of occasions before, ironically, swapping roles with Steve Evans when he took over as manager of Rotherham when Steve left there to go to Leeds.

Ronnie Reid - player and coach for Boston United

A miscellany of memories

I can't swim. But there was one occasion when I regretted not taking the opportunity to learn - and it was all connected with an FA Cup t ie. United were drawn away to Kettering Town when they were one of the best non -League clubs in the country.

We gave it the big match treatment and, although it was only a 60-mile journey to play The Poppies, we travelled overnight and stayed at the George Hotel, in St amfo rd. On the Saturday morning, before moving on to Kettering, the players trained on The Green, near the river in Stamford. When finishing their light workout, they were still in high spirits and decided to throw me in the river! It was only when I was struggling in the water that they heeded my pleas that I could not sw im, and they quickly pulled me out. I was gasping for breath and a little scared.

The lads went on to secure a fine 3-1 win, with John Moyes scoring a cracker, in one of the few games Kevin Hector played for United.

This was one ofthe incidents I recalled while delving into the depths of my mind to re-live the major stories from my many years with Boston United. It was one of several offbeat items that surfaced. Perhaps they could be described as a potpourri of gossip, or miscellany of memories. I will share some more of them with you...

Sam Allardyce hit the headlines when he was appointed manager of England, and again when he left 53 days later under controversial circumstances. I met him when he was manager of Bolton Wanderers, and David Norris moved there from United for a fee of £50,000 . Steve Evans was also present but, for some reason I never understood, we went in separate cars and I had to drive alone to the new stadium at Bolton to complete the paperwork with their secretary, Simon Marland .

Sam invited me in to chat about David and I found him to be a nice guy, a proper football man. He arranged for me to have a conducted tour of the facilities. His son Craig later came to United as a player.

When the majority of the United directors resigned at the end of the 1976 season when the club was rejected by the Football League because the ground was deemed not to be up to standard (Wigan Athletic were elected instead of United), there was only treasurer Alf Bell and myself left to run the club. My wife Maureen and I represented the club at the Northern Premier League annual meeting held at the Daresbury Hotel, Cheshi re. A few weeks later the directors returned to office.

The Chairman Mr Ernest Malkinson decided that we needed to raise money to build new stands to develop the ground , so we were one of the first clubs in the country to have it's own lottery with a £1000 first prize. This was a really successful fund raising initiative and continued to be for many years until the National Lottery came into being . We all worked really hard to make this a success and so did many of the supporters who were agents, selling the tickets on behalf of the football club.

During the period that York Street was being re-developed, we had built the Spayne Road and Town End stands but we played without the main stan d. Dugouts were on the land where the new stand was scheduled to be built. We decided that, during the summer, we would have sheep grazing the pitch to save the trouble of cutting it. There was a wire fence around the touchline to keep them in.

Maureen and I were newly married and living in a flat in Main Ridge when, early one Sunday morning, I received a call from the police to say that our sheep had gone for a walk, someone had taken the fence down. I found them roaming around Field Street and at the side of Eagles fish shop. I had to round them up and drive them back to the ground, and then find someone to help me fence them in again.

It wasn't one of the best of ideas we came up with because we had to clear up their mess on a regular basis!

Another occasion I received a call from the police was when the B&Q store caught fire, and the football club's stand was too close for comfort. I had to open the stadium to allow access for the emergency services.

The Fire Brigade sprayed the back of the stand with water while asbestos was coming off the stand onto the pit ch. Photographers were climbing the floodlights to gain a vantage point to take their pictures.

Chairman Pat Malkinson was called out and I remember that he drove his car on land between the stand and B&Q, but then had to leave it at the far end of the ground until the following day because it was so hot and unsafe. Contractors had to clear asbestos off the pitch where some of the grass had been badly burned.

When United won the Premier Division of the Southern League in season 1999-2000, it was decided to hold the league's annual meeting on a ferry in Felixstowe harbour on a Saturday afte rnoon . Then the ferry set sail for Hamburg to spend Saturday night and Sunday there, before sailing back, the dinner and presentations being held while at sea before arriving back at Felixstowe at lunch time on Monday.

Most difficult problem I had that weekend was transporting the winner's shield, which is the biggest trophy in English football. It took up the whole of the back of my estate car, and then there was the struggle to get it on and off the ferry.

There was a time when the York Street pitch was likely to become very wet and soggy. This was before modern drainage equipment took a lot of graft out of the remedial work, and the digging to put in new drains had to be done by hand.

The first time all the hard work was done by long-standing supporter Ron Butler (a local goalkeeper of some repute) and his brother Bernard. Once we used a trailer hitched to director Sydney Malkinson's Hillman car to haul soil and stones across the pitch. Later, when we had a flooding problem on the centre circle, we decided to dig it out and pipe it ourselves, with the help of two North Sea Camp inmates, and the heavy involvement of Chairman Pat Malkinson and his son Andrew. There has been no problem since.

York Street, as well as being home to Boston United, used to host many other events, and boost the takings at the Social Club at the same time. Held there was the finish to the Skegness to Boston Seabank Marathon, and we also hosted three American Football matches after being assured that they would be a big attraction, but few spectators turned up.

Incidentally, I played a part in helping Gilbert Sands and George Wheatman, plus other keen sports people, start the marathon. Gilbert was the main instigator and the event was originally aimed at raising money for the Boston and District Youth Football League, another of Gilbert's ideas. I was one of the party "sweeping up" at the first marathon, that is walking at the back to make sure no-one was left behind, or being of assistance to anyone in difficulties. That was a long day!

On another occasion I took part and finished 345th out of about 1,000 competitors.

Local soccer players loved playing at York Street (it was their Wembley) in league and county cup finals. Now they go elsewhere.

Another outstanding occasion for me was when I represented the club at the centenary FA Cup final dinner in 1981 at the Royal Lancaster Hotel in London, a representative of each competing club being invited. The next day I watched Tottenham Hotspurs and Manchester City draw 1-1, after extra time, in a match refereed by Keith Hackett who cut his teeth in Northern Premier League football, being a frequent visitor to Boston . He also refereed the replay, again at Wembley, when Spurs won 3-2.

The strongest man in English professional football is reputed to be Adebayo

Akinfenwa, whose host of clubs include Boston United . As I write this he is still, at the age of 34, banging in the goals for the likes AFC Wimbledon and, later, Wycombe Wanderers.

I had to look up to him when I signed him in 2003 because he was a mountain of a man, but he was not all brute force; he could play a bit too. He did not stay long at York Street because the train trip from his London home proved a bit too much and he played, I think, just four games for United, scoring one goal.

The last time I saw him he was hurling himself out of my car. He had played in a reserve game and asked me to take him to meet his girl friend at McDonald's, near the railway station. We were driving, in traffic, when all of a sudden he opens the car door and jumps out. He had spotted his girl friend walking down the road and ran off to meet her, leaving the car door open in the middle of the road! I have never seen him in person since, but I have seen quite a bit of him on television, and he always causes something of a stir. Maureen still has his shirt. It had to be pretty big to fit him - and to carry his name .

Another visitor to York Street I have seen on television, often and in elite company, is Martin O'Neill, the Republic of Ireland manager and frequently a TV pundit. It was during the time that the ex-Grantham boss was manager at Wycombe Wanderers when he called to see a match after driving all the way from Hartlepool where he had watched a game in the afternoon - an example of the many miles managers from the lower leagues travel in search of players and watching opponent s.

Moreover he had with him his wife and their two babies and asked Maureen if she could help change their nappies while he watched the match. Of course she was only too willing to help, one of the many jobs she has been called to do at Boston United.

Perhaps it is a visit that Martin remembers because he got lost on the way into Boston, was caught speeding at Wyberton, and was late for the match. I have often wondered if he felt his visit was worthwhile.

Non-League football has always been, and still is, my major interest, and I am an avid reader of the Non-League weekly newspaper.

I was privileged to witness at first hand the historical milestone which led to the creation of the Alliance Premier League, the forerunner to the present day National League. Along with Ernest and Pat Malkinson, and George Wheatman, then Editor of the Boston Standard, I attended the meeting which launched the new competition at the famous Cafe Royal in London.

This was preceded, on the Friday evening, by an inaugural dinner which was memorable by the reaction of Mr Ernest to the wine list when he spotted the price of a particular vintage which was being sold for about £2 a bottle at the Gliderdrome but cost something like £30 at the Cafe Royal. The look on his face remains more memorable than the important outcome of the weekend.

Elected President of the new APL was the so-called "stormy petrel" of the game at that time, Burnley butcher Bob Lord, vice-President of the Football League who held their AGM at the same venue on Friday. He told representatives of non-League clubs that the old pals' act was protecting clubs which had "let the Football League down time and time again." He hoped the new APL could become the Fifth Division of the League in the not too distant future.

Boston United received a brusque "Good luck for the new season" from Mr Lord as the four of us shared the lift with himontheway out of the meeting.

This was in the summer of 1979, and a few weeks later the new league was in operation made up of teams from the Southern and Northern Premier Leagues, plus Bangor City, the only team from Wales. The inaugural teams were AP Leamington, Altrincham, Bangor City, Barnett, Barrow, Bath City, Boston United, Gravesend and Northfleet, Kettering Town, Maidstone United, Northwich Victoria, Nuneaton Borough, Redditch United, Scarborough, Stafford Rangers, Telford United, Wealdstone, Weymouth, Worcester City and Yeovil Town.

It is interesting to reflect on the varying fortunes of this group of clubs over the years. Boston United is not alone in having had a bumpy ride.

Altrincham, relegated from the National League North last season, were the first champions. Runners-up were Weymouth, and Worcester City third. United were fourth and it was obviously their away form that cost them a higher placing as they lost eight times on their travels, while they were beaten only once at Fortress York Street.

Back in 1983 -August to be more precise- I shared the disappointment and dismay of United directors when local magistrates, chaired by Coun Alf Goodson, refused permission for the Social Club to have a drinks licence after matches from 4.45 pm to 5.30pm. Police had objected to the application, and the magistrates upheld the submission of solicitor, the late Stuart Treharne, that ordinary league matches were not special occasions to justify granting the licence.

We were baffled by the decision as we were able to enjoy an after-match drink at other clubs we visited up and down the country. Of course, licensing laws were much tougher in those days, compared with nowadays when you can buy alcohol almost round the clock.

I still have a cutting from the Boston Standard dated 10th November 1978. It is a report of a meeting of Boston Borough Council whose members had before them a recommendation, from their own Development Control Committee, that they should refuse the first £200, 000 phase of improvements at York Street.

Nine residents from around the ground had signed a petition opposing the height of the proposed covering of the Spayne Road terracing, and their objection was supported by the Fydell Rowley Residents Association.

But 16 local residents had signed a petition supporting the ground improvements, while another petition of support was signed by 4,102 people, presumably United fans.

Councillors, perhaps with an eye on not upsetting the majority of voters, turned the committee decision on its head, and gave the go-ahead for the plans, with 20 councillors voting in favour.

One job I really enjoyed was liaising with top clubs to arrange fixtures, and sample their professionalism. This happened twice in the pre-season of 2001 when we had practice matches against both Manchester United, who attracted a full house to York Street, and Liverpool. Both clubs sent teams of mainly young players, but there was a lot of talent on view, and it was a compliment to Boston United that they agreed to come. I had a sense of pride just being involved.

During my time at Boston United I saw a number of players leave the club and bring in sizeable amounts of cash in transfer fees. Julian Joachim's reputed £100,000 move to Darlington was the bigge st . Next was the £50,000 received from Bolton Wanderers for David Norris. Greg Fee £20,000 to Sheffield Wednesday. Gordon Simmonite was transferred to Blackpool for £15,000 , and a similar fee was received from Kettering Town for Mickey Nuttell.

After playing only one pre-season game, Brendan Phillips was sold to Mansfield Town for £10,000!

On the other side of the coin, United paid Worksop £10,000 for Martin Hardy, £5,000 to Frickley for Paul Shirtliffe, we also paid Barnet £5,000 for goalkeeper Kevin Blackwell, and £2,000 in their first deal with Boston Town for Mark Cox. These were all in the late 70's and early 80's ...which was quite a lot of money in those days!

When I attended United's home game against Salford City on Saturday March 25th

107

2017, I noticed that there was a David Norris in the visiting team - but I didn't realise that it was the same man who had been transferred from United to Bolton until thegame started.

Afterwards we met up for a chat and spoke about him joining the Trotters, and his career that took in Ipswich Town, Plymouth Argyle, Leeds United and Blackpool, and his return to live in Bolton and his signing for Salford - a journey that had taken 17 years. He returned to TheJakemans in 2018 atthe

John and David Norris meeting up again for the first time since his move to Bolton Wanderers

age of 37 and played a few games for The Pilgrims, but has now moved on to pastures new.

It was enough to make a vicar blush - and that is just what it did when the Rev John Moore was found with "stolen" cutlery in his pockets. It was when United travelled to Merthyr Tydfil and stayed overnight at a hotel in the t own. During a pre-match meal, Steve Adams, who was ever the practical joker, filled the coat pockets of the Rev John with cutlery, and salt and pepper pots - and then told hotel staff that he thought the club Chaplain was attempting to steal them. When he was asked to turn out his pockets no one was more surprised to see what was in them than the vicar.

The wing wizard and fantastic character Steve Adams with striker Paul Cavell

Sadly the mischievous Steve Adams died in March 2017, after a long illness, Chris Cook and I went along to his funeral in Sheffield. There were 17 ex-United players and officials among the 500 mourners. Steve played more than 100 times for United and was highly rated as a "flair player."

A character I met while on my travels with United was the famous Uri Geller, better known for the mystery of how he could bend spoons without any obvious contact, than he was for being chairman of Exeter City. It was in his latter capacity that we met and he gave us an exhibition of his spoon-bending skills, while also talking a lot about his friend, Michael Jackson.

Local players who made the grade

Boston United have brought in players from all over the country. They have flown in from Scotland, travelled by train from London, and criss-crossed motorways from east and west. But what about homegrown talent?

Despite its rural nature, Lincolnshire is a hive of sporting activity, and Boston is one of the hot-spots.

Football, I am sure, is the most popular. Boston and District Saturday Football League is the largest of its kind in the county, and there are also a number of youth teams playing in the Mid-Lines Youth League as well as in leagues in the Peterborough area.

Boston United also has a very strong youth set-up currently being run by Lee Mitchell, plus community sides and the newly-formed ladies' set-up at the Jakemans Stadium.

Only disappointment is the demise, in recent seasons, of the Boston Sunday League, especially after the battle to get it established many years ago in the face of opposition from those who did not agree with Sunday football, and councillors who did not want Borough Council pitches used on Sunday.

Perhaps, also, there is mild regret from the present owners of the Pilgrims that progress from the youth sides to the first team squad has been disappointing. Hopefully that will change in the not too distant future.

Surprisingly, despite the number of youngsters playing football regularly in the area, few have made the grade at the highest level.

Former United manager, Jim Smith, was once heard to say that Lincolnshire is too laid back to produce good footballers. "You can stroll across the streets of Boston, whereas you have to dash across in the cities," he said.

Nevertheless there are some with Boston United connections who readily come to mind after joining the elite.

One is now retired solicitor Mike Pinner, an outstanding goalkeeper at Boston Grammar School and with Boston Boys. He went on play more than 100 times for England amateurs, and was a member of the famous Pegasus amateur side.

But he also tasted the professional game with Boston United and, at the very top, Manchester United as well as other Football League clubs. This was in the 1950s and 60s. He played for Notts County before he was 16.

Gordon Bolland's is a name that always comes to mind when you think of local talent who made a career out of football. A product of my old play area, the Burgess Pit, in Boston's Freiston Road, it was a life-changing leap for him when he left sleepy Boston to move to London and join Chelsea. He became a regular first teamer at Stamford Bridge, before moving on to Millwall and Norwich City. He was a popular player for both teams, and soccer fans who are also television viewers with a long memory will remember a breakaway goal he took so calmly to clinch a surprise win for the Canaries against Manchester United, at Old Trafford.

Gordon ended his football career back at York Street where, despite being hampered by the wear and tear full-time football had taken on his knees, he still showed more than a few glimpses of his sublime skill. Today he earns his living as a taxi driver in the tow n.

Three other players who started climbing the football ladder at the highly successful Wyberton youth set-up, and also have had Boston United connections, were Mick Vinter, Ian Nimmo and Julian Joachim.

Mick, a striker during Jim Smith's management days, moved on to Notts County where he became a prolific goalscorer and stayed there for several seasons. Later he followed Jim to Oxford United, and returned to York Street at the end of his career, having also played for Wrexham, Mansfield Town, Matlock Town, Oakham United and Hucknall Town. After football, he became an insurance salesman.

Ian Nimmo was a prolific goalgetter in youth football before moving to Sheffield Wednesday where he made it into the first team managed by Jack Charlton. He later joined former United player-manager Dave Cusack at Doncaster Rovers, where he suffered a broken leg. He showed his love for the game by turning out locally when he returned to Boston where he has been a driving instructor for many years.

One of the biggest talents to leave Boston since Gordon Bolland was Julian Joachim, a pupil at Kitwood Boys School. I remember when United hosted all the local schools finals at York Street and, when he was player-manager, Dave Cusack always made a point of watching these games. On the occasion I recall, Dave drooled over the performance of one Kitwood player who ran the opposition ragged in the final of the Pitcher Cup, and scored a hatful of goals. Yes, that player was Julian Joachim.

Julian went on to have a wonderful career in the professional game, first with Leicester City, where he won England youth and under 21 caps, and then at Aston Villa in the Premier League.

110

During the five years we played in Division Two, Steve Evans persuaded Julian to come to play for United and he was still capable of scoring goals. He played 49 times for Boston.

He was subsequently transferred to Darlington for a fee that was reputed to be £100,000, and later turned out for United Counties League teams.

He was one of the ex-players who found time to surprise me by attending my farewell function, and is now involved with the Find a Jewel agency. Let's hope he discovers a young player as talented as he was.

One player I was delighted to help on the way to soccer stardom, although he never played for United, was Simon Garner, a former pupil at Boston Grammar School.

In my early days of running Real Towell, Towell FC and their youth teams, I became very friendly with his dad, Geoff (Gandy) Garner, and his mother Peg. The family lived in Field Street, and Geoff was manager of Boston FC youth team, our arch rivals.

Every Sunday evening in the football season we used to meet up at the Main Ridge laundrette to wash the teams' kit and chew over the day's football gossip . Always with Geoff was his youngest son, Simon.

As a result, I followed Simon's progress in school, county and local football and, indeed, eventually played alongside him in the Lincolnshire Standard

Simon Garner

Sunday team with the likes of Rob Singleton (former Sports Editor of the Lincolnshire Echo and Deputy Editor of the Boston Target), Bob Whitaker (well-known as the local television cameraman), Graham Brown, Brian "Bimbo" Lake, and my brother-in-law Graham Fo rman. Simon was the youngest in the team by many years, and scored goals for fun. He was nicknamed Gutsy Garner I was so impressed that, when Jim Smith took the job as manager at Blackburn Rovers, I persuaded him to give Simon a trial. He did so well that Jim signed him on contract, and he went on to become the Rovers' record goalscorer, and a big favourite at Ewood Park.

When Simon signed for the Rovers, Maureen travelled with him and his mum and dad to Blackburn to renew our friendship with the Smiths. On another occasion, Simon invited me, Pat Malkinson and his son Andrew to watch him play in a cup quarter final at Ewood Park. Jim Smith had moved on by then but spearheading the Blackburn attack alongside Simon that day was a former Boston United favourite, Bobby Svare.

We were given a warm welcome and the best of hospitality in the directors' lounge. On one occasion, when Blackburn beat Derby County 5-1, Simon scored all five goals. He went on to play for West Bromwich Albion and Wycombe Wanderers, and, whenever Boston United played at Adams Park, the home of Wycombe Wanderers, Simon always sought me out to talk about old times. Unfortunately, Geoff and Peg have passed away now, and I have not spoken to Simon for a long time, but I understand that he still lives near Wycombe and works as a painter and decorator. I still meet his older brother David, however, as he is a relative to David Whalley, partner to our daughter Lisa. It still gives me a warm feeling that I helped Simon onto the ladder of a successful football career.

It was well-known, and sometimes commented upon in the national Press, that Simon was a smoker, and had been from an early age. Football folklore tells the story of how he was caught having a cigarette by Blackburn's youth team coach, and despatched to the manager for a suitable reprimand. Jim Smith's reaction - and I quite believe this, knowing the man so well -was to tell him to go away, and be more careful in the future. "Don't let him catch you," was the advice.

His liking for a fag didn't stop Simon scoring goals and, with 192 of them from 1978 to 1991, he is still the highest scorer in Blackburn Rovers' 140-year history.

Another Bostonian and former Pilgrim who did not move into the Football League, but did represent England at schoolboy level, is Mick Lyon, who moved to College football in America and went on to become a very well known coach in Ladies Football. Mick played at right back for United as a teenager under the management of Arthur Mann, he played 39 times for United first team, and was sub eight times. Mick still lives in North America but unfortunately Multiple Sclerosis has afflicted him for over ten years now and he is in a wheelchair, but still has a big smile like he always had.

Defender Matt Hocking trained with United at Newark as a schoolboy, before becoming a professional with Sheffield United, Hull City and York City. During this period he made 154 League appearances. He was brought back by Steve Evans to play for United and made his debut in our first League Two match against Bournemouth, and went on to play 67 games, plus nine appearances as substitute. Later he joined the club's Football in the Community project, before leaving to continue the same kind of work with Peterborough United.

Tom Hopper, whose family have run a jewellers business in Boston Market Place for a number of generations, is another striker who first showed his promise at Boston Grammar School and with the Boston United Centre of Excellence where he did so well when playing for the Pilgrims Under 18 team in the FA Youth Cup.

He impressed sufficiently to be included in United's first team squad, and became the youngest player ever to turn out for the first team. While doing all this, Tom attracted the attention of scouts from a higher level, and was snatched away from us by Leicester City (without any compensation) where he made it into the first team, and became a regular squad member. His association with theFoxes came to an end after a much publicised incident involving a trio of young players while on tour with theclub in Thailand.

Tom then went on to play in Division One with Scunthorpe United where ex-Pilgrim Jim Rodwell is chief executive, but recently he signed for Southend United and is still scoring goals so will hopefully work his way back up the football ladder.

Back at York Street at the start of the 2016-17 season was young forward, Liam Adams, another product of BUFC Centre of Excellence, who joined Nottingham Forest on a two-year apprenticeship.

One talented local player who became a legend in the town turned down the chance to join a Football League club to stay loyal to Boston United . That player was the ever-popular Chris Cook, a former pupil at Kitwood Boys School, now a director at York Street.

Chris's goal-getting exploits with the Pilgrims caught the attention of Colin Murphy, when he was manager at Lincoln City, and he was keen to have the Boston player in the Imps' line-up . I am sure Chris would have been a big success at League level had he not rejected this offer. We shall never know how full-time training would have lifted his game to an even higher level than that which served Boston United so well over a number of years, and which included a goal at Wembley.

Chris was four short of playing 400 games for United, and was substitute on 88 occasions, while scoring a club record 181 times. What the club would give now for such a local "find".

Chris was not only a successful non -League footballer, but has also made a success off the field of play as a businessman.

I remember going to Kitwood Boys School to sign him so that he could travel with the first team, and take that first step towards becoming a local icon. It was not always easy for Chris playing for his home-town team, and I remember the usually easygoing Albert Phelan becoming angry at the barracking Chris suffered from some fans during a pre-season county cup defeat against Grantham. Albert hit back at these fans in the local Press. "Chris is a lad with potential," he said. "But the only way he can improve is by playing at the highest level. He wants games and experience.

"He made mistakes on Saturday just the same as any other beginner will make mistakes, but I thought he played quite well. He missed a couple of chances and, because of this and the unfair criticism, he was very dejected after the match. "He will have to toughen up and shrug this off, but I would have thought the Boston supporters would have been delighted that we were giving a chance to a local player. I can't understand them." No doubt those critics would have changed their attitude when Chris went on to become the club's record goalscorer.

Another record Chris must have achieved is the number of changes in hairstyle that I have spotted when trawling through my scrapbooks!

Another product of the prolific Wyberton Colts was midfielder Steve Appleby who became a big favourite of the York Street fans, so much so that he was twice voted Player of the Year - in seasons 1994-95 and 1997-98. He was also Players' Player of the Year in the season between, and these awards represented a wonderful spell for Steve.

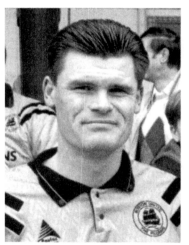

His work ethic really appealed to the supporters and he made 239 appearances for the first team, plus 11 as substitute. As a schoolboy, Steve scored more than 100 goals for Wyberton Colts. He came to Boston after playing for Kettering Town in the Conference and captaining Bourne Town in the United Counties League.

**Fans favourite midfielder
Steve Appleby**

Subsequently he played for Wyberton, Holbeach and Spalding, and managed Bourne Town. Last I heard he was still playing locally at the age of around 50, such was his love for the game.

Signed from Lincolnshire League Skegness Town in July 1996, after impressing in pre-season trials, Simon Armstrong played 55 times for United's first team, at one point moving to Port Vale.

He was a member of the England Schools Under 18 squad during the 1996-97 season, returned on loan at the end of that season, and later also played for Gainsborough Trinity and Boston Town. Unfortunately, progress had not continued and the earlier promise did not blossom and he decided to go to University.

Another promising youngster who emerged through the youth team was Alex Beck who made his first team debut at the age of 17, but he played only three more times, although he was substitute on 11 occasions. He was released in 2009.

One more local youngster to emerge from United's Centre of Excellence, which he joined from Grimsby Town in 2005, was Lee Beeson who made his first team debut against Solihull Moors in 2007, but, again, he did not maintain the momentum.

Although born in Wyberton, and playing Boston League football for Tumby Woodside, it wasn't until he had experienced League football with seven clubs (Derby County, Halifax, Sheffield Wednesday, Barnsley, Lincoln City, Chesterfield and Scunthorpe) that striker Derek Bell came to York Street. He did not stay long, playing just nine first team games, and being used as substitute seven times, but he chipped in with five goals. He had gone to Derby straight from school.

Early in my days with United, there was a young Lincolnshire lad brought to the club by Jim Smith who had known him at Lincoln City. Robbie Coates, who was at the club between 1970 and 1973, always seemed to do well when called into the first team and scored 11 goals in his 25 games. He could play in midfield or up front and, at the age of 15, had become the youngest player to turn out for Spalding United first team.

It took a fee of £6,000 to bring Boston-born Mark Cook into the York Street fold. He was 19 years old when the midfielder came on loan in 1989, and impressed. He had joined Lincoln City from school as a YTS trainee, and made one League appearance for the Imps. He played 41 games for United.

One local lad who made a stunning start for United was Anthony Elding. He scored with a header just 32 seconds into his debut in a Nationwide Variety Club Trophy match. Anthony was a graduate of the United Academy and had two spells with the club in the early naughties. In that time he scored 12 goals in 36 games, and made 27 appearances as a substitute.

His best time in football was probably at Stevenage where he scored 54 goals in 118 appearances, but he was also top scorer at Stockport County, and had spells at a number of other clubs, including Kettering Town, Leeds United and Crewe Alexandra. Last I heard, he was playing and living in Ireland.

115

Another Lincolnshire-born player who was a favourite of the fans was defender Joby Gowshall. They voted him "Player of the Year" in season 2000-01 . He had been with Grimsby Town and Lincoln City before joining United . He played 178 games for The Pilgrims but moved to Gainsborough after failing to agree terms for the 01-02 season. Later he played for Kings Lynn and Grantham, and returned to BUFC to play for the reserves . Outside of football, he joined the Fire Service.

One of the best goalkeepers to emerge from Boston, in my opinion, is John McPherson, a rival of mine for a place in school and county teams. He may have been deemed to be on the small side by those who prefer their goalkeepers to be big and bulky, but he had a safe pair of hands, was agile, brave and an excellent shot-stopper.

He was United's No 2 goalkeeper in the year we went to Wembley and stood in for Kevin Blackwell when he had a cartilage operat ion . One of the games he played was the first one on the road to Wembley, away to Alvechurch. He played eight first team games in the 1984-85 season, and turned out a total of 20 times for the first team.

A college lecturer, some of his best years were with Boston FC, and he also played for Skegness Town and Holbeach United as well as being the regular goalkeeper for Lincolnshire, over many years and many games. In Sunday football he played for the formidable Gipsey Bridge side put together by the equally formidable Gilbert Sands.

Members of the Nuttell family have been prominent in Boston sporting circles, and two of them, brothers Derek and Micky, have played a lot of first team football for United.

Derek, a plumber by trade and product of United Reserves and local football, was the first on the scene. A classy defender , he could also play in midfield or up front. Whatever task he was asked to perform, he did a good, wholehearted job. Although he did not play at Wembley, he was part of the first team squad that year and, between 1983 and 1988, he played 124 first team games. He also played for Worksop Town, Spalding United and Kings Lynn. He has latterly been heavily involved with theBUFC Centre of Excellence.

Former Boston Grammar School pupil, Micky was an old-fashioned type of centre forward, physical and good in the air, and was much-travelled during his soccer career .

He had four different spells at York Street and, ironically, it took a fee of £14 , 000 to bring him to his hometown club for the first time when he was signed from Wycombe Wanderers in 1991. He was sold to Kettering Town at the end of that

116

season, before moving on to Rushden and Diamonds where he was top scorer in 1993-94.

Other clubs Micky played for included Peterborough United, Cheltenham, Dagenham and Redbridge , Burton Albion, Kings Lynn, Bedford Town, Wisbech, Holbeach and Spalding. He played 92 games for Boston United and scored 14 goals.
Not born in Boston, but a Lincolnshire lad through and through, is Darren Munton, a prolific goalscorer who moved to York Street from Bourne to earn a regular first team spot. His son Zak, another striker who knows where the goal is, has played for United'sunder 21 team .

Although born in Swineshead and attending school in Donington , Andrew Stanhope joined Boston United from Peterborough, to become a valued member of the first team. He played 180 games, and was substitute 32 times, between 1996 and 2001, when he scored 27 goals. Later he played for Kings Lynn and Spalding United.

A number of young local lads progressed from the Academy or Reserves to get a taste of first team football, players like Mark Melson who played 34 times, plus 29 appearances as sub, between 1995 and 2000.

Midfielder Adam Milson, born in Skegness, and voted Player of the Year in 2008, a midfielder who played 31 times (16) and scored five goals.

Leigh Taylor who made his first team debut at the age of 16 and went on to play four first team games (16) before moving on to Holbeach, Spalding and Bourne, a well-trodden path for local players.

Utility player Neil Timby who made seven (11) first team appearances .

Lincolnshire county schoolboy striker Paul Watts, from Skegness, who notched 23 goals from 60 games (49), later playing for Gainsborough, Kings Lynn and Spal ding.

Ollie Ryan was born in Boston but joined Lincoln City as a youngster where he impressed in the reserves and was always talked about as a good prospect, but had few first team chances with the Imps. He was top scorer for United, with 22 goals, when he signed for season 2008-09. He played 37 games (1) despite missing the last two months of the season with a bad ankle injury.

One product of local football who played only six first team games for United but will be remembered fondly for a sensational performance in that 0-0 FA Cup draw at Derby County, is goalkeeper Nigel Simpson (1971-75).

117

He made his first team debut against Macclesfield Town, at the age of 17, and saved a penalty from one of the showmen of non-League football, the unforgettable Brian Fidler, who later became a United player.

One recent product of the BUFC Centre of Excellence was former Boston Grammar School student, Harry Limb, from Old Leake. He played for United in the FA Youth Cup and, after his 16th birthday, was included in the first team squad, unfortunately manager Dennis Greene didn't really fancy him enough to give him any appearances from the bench even though he was sub quite a few times!

At the end of season 2015-16, he left York Street to join Wisbech Town, where he made a big impression, so much so that League scouts became interested. I watched him on behalf of Swansea City and was so impressed that I arranged for him to have a trial there. Although he was not signed, his potential was acknowledged. Burnley were more receptive and they offered him a contract when he finished his A Levels. So season 2017-18 saw Harry launch his bid to become a professional footballer.

Another local who has had an outstanding career in top-class football, but has not been connected with Boston United, is Danny Butterfield. I often saw his mum who worked at the bank where I did club business, and I have always followed his career with interest.

Former pupil at Boston Grammar School, Danny joined Grimsby Town as a youth and, between 1997 and 2002, made 124 League appearances for the Mariners. Then he moved to Crystal Palace where he became a popular figure with the fans, especially on the occasion when, as a makeshift striker, he responded with a hat-trick in a 3-1 FA Cup fourth round replay win over Wolves. The three goals came inside 6 minutes 48 seconds-a left footer, right footer and a header.

Danny also played for Charlton, Southampton, Bolton and Exeter and, in total, made 569 first-class appearances, truly a fine career, first as a midfielder but mainly as a full-back. Now he is making his way in coaching, and is a coach of Premier League Southampton's under 18 team.

This is a look back at some of the local players who have made their mark on the game, some either knocking on the York Street door before moving on, or have been seen on the Boston soccer scene.

Progress from spongeman

Many old footballers will shudder at memories of the spongeman, euphemistically called the trainer. I became one when Peter Jackson, erstwhile holder of the title, left the club, and this match-day role was added to my many other tasks Because I wore a tracksuit, and football boots to enable a sprint to any injury crisis, I was a step up from many of the spongemen who could be seen in village football - men often wearing wellingtons, a flat cap and puffing at a cigarette, but carrying the compulsory bucket of water and sponge, and sometimes a bottle of smelling salts, all that was deemed necessary to tend the wide range of injuries that could be suffered in any football match.

I carried similar equipment, and was blessed with as little medical knowledge as most volunteers. My how things have changed-thank goodness.

In the early seventies, United did not have a physiotherapist ready and waiting on the touchline to give a prompt diagnosis of any injury and, if the spongeman's shock tactics did not work the miracle, the player had to wait until later for assessment from Bill Watt.

Now, I hasten to add, Bill, whose availability had been secured by manager Jim Smith, was a well respected physio who held private clinics around the county, including one day a week at York Street, and was associated with theBritish Cycling Association, but he did not do the matchday work of the present experts.

In the case of serious injury, an ambulance was summoned. There was no doctor on hand, although representatives of the St John Ambulance Brigade were usually present to provide some level of comfort.

After being appointed club secretary, I had other duties at matches and a new trainer had to be found, and we persuaded Frank Scrupps, a plasterer by trade who was handily placed living in nearby Spayne Road, to take on the role.

He was succeeded by Don Robinson, who moved over from Boston FC, and he had the honour of running out onto the hallowed turf at Wembley in the 1985 FA Challenge Trophy final.

As the focus became more fixed on matters medical, an experienced physiotherapist was brought in. He was the highly-rated Ted Goddard, from Sheffield, who brought with himPaul Smith, son of the England physio at the time, Alan Smith, the top man in football.

They were available for pre-match massages, and able to give a quick assessment of the severity of injurie s. With their early intervention and treatment it often meant that players would not play on to aggravate injuries, and would be available more quickly to return to playing.

This pair were followed by Dave Baldwin, who was serving in the RAF at Digby. He was so good that he was snapped up by Norwich City, so it is not only players who are in demand .

Another man from Nocton Hall, Scotsman Bill Mackay followed Dave, and was also excellent at his job . Born at Greenock, he had been the physio for the England rugby team, and lived at Metheringham .

Jim Woods, brother of former England goalkeeper, Chris, was another top, thoroughly professional, physiotherapist who served the club well before a disagreement with manager Evans prompted him to concentrate on his own practice . Jim had been in the Prison Service before changing profession, and is well known for his annual trip to Wimbledon to use his physiotherapy skills on some of the top players in the tennis world. He still works from his home in Kirton End.

At the time we became full-time, and earned promotion to Division Two, we needed a full-time physiotherapist and Steve Evans brought in Essex-based Lee Taylor, who had been with Leyton Orient and Dagenham and Redbridge. Lee, who was son of the subsequent United manager, Tommy Taylor, was very good and also helped with nutrition and sports science.

He received a helping hand from a Boston girl who was studying for her degree at Huddersfield University, and that was the best thing he could have done for Boston United. That student was Katie Cooper and, ten years later, she was still in post when I retired. She has, however, resigned since after finding that demanding arrangements under a new manager meant that she was taking too much time from her own sports injury business.

When she rang to tell me of her decision, I felt that it was a big blow for the club. She was the best physiotherapist I had worked with.

Katie took on the responsibility when Lee left the Pilgrims to see service at Notts County, in New Zealand and India, and Preston North End and Mansfield Town where he was reunited with Steve Evans in November 2016.

She has been a joy to work with, attending all training sessions and dealing with all medical issues within the club, as well as running her own Treatment of Injuries business in the town A fitness instructor, Katie has completed the London Marathon, and competes in 5 and 10k races.

She is also a sports therapist, and organised and supervised recovery programmes for injured players, working with them in the gymnasium, on the track and in the swimming pool. Katie has been a special person in my life at BUFC and is as far removed from the spongeman that I was long ago as you can imagine.

Along the road of better health supervision for playing staff, qualified medical practitioners have also become part of the Boston United set-up.

The first Medical Officer at the club, long before promotion to the Football League, was the late Dr Laurence Taffinder, from Sibsey Surgery. Later, one of his colleagues from Stickney, Dr Thomas Busch, held the position for a long time. The current club doctor is Dr Turki.

Another aspect of club life that has changed dramatically involves health and safet y. Gone are the days when there were no safety officers, no safety advisory group and few, if any, stewards. All this changed with the arrival of League football when health and safety became a very important part of the regime, and an additional cost.

A safety advisory group was formed and met every month in the early days, later to be reduced to three or four times a year. It is made up of representatives from the club, police, fire brigade, ambulance se rvice, supporters' association, and Civil Defence . All kinds of safety issues are discussed, and inspections carried out to ensure that necessary repairs are carried out, standards are maintained and supporters can attend matches in a safe environment.

Safety, and supporters' comfort, will be in the forefront of the minds of people planning the new Boston United ground as part of the massive Quadrant development. It will, of course, in many ways, be sad to leave the stadium which has been the home of the club since 1934, but a new purpose-built home for the club can become a major asset for the area.

It was, therefore, in my new role as club President, following my retirement, that I was particularly interested in visiting the new, much-admired, facilities at fellow National League North club, AFC Fylde. As we emerged from the snow and sleet, what an impressive sight greeted us at Wesham, just off Junction 3 of the M55. It was Fylde's new Mill Farm Sports Village - a world away from their old ground which was littered with Po rtacabin s.

Adjacent to the new stadium was an Aldi supermarket, and the frontage to the ground was, to say the least, highly impressive.

Helping to carry the kit from the coach, we entered the most magnificent away dressing room I have ever seen in non-League football and, believe me, I have seen a lot. But nothing like this. Along with ex-manager Dennis Greene's partner, Carla George, and United fans, Mick Small and partner Donna Harrison, who had travelled the previous evening, we enjoyed coffee in a lounge at the front of the stadium. I was amazed at the number of supporters who were in there, eating, drinking and watching Manchester United v Arsenal and Forest Green v Lincoln City, on massive television screens.

Upstairs we joined other BUFC officials on a tour of the facilities - ten executive boxes, two restaurants, all better than anything I had ever seen in semi-professional football, although facilities were pretty good at Rushden and Diamonds and Darlington before both these clubs came crashing down.

The journey to the game was in horrible weather, the trip home was equally bad, the result, a 9-2 thrashing, was depressing, but none of this could remove from my mind the initiative AFC Fylde had shown in developing such superb facilities, with a team to match.

I wondered - and have been wondering since-whether Boston United will be able to match this dream development, and whether they will be able to field a top-class side to match it? We can only hope.

Embracing the community

One aspect of my time with United which gives me a sense of pride is the manner in which the club embraced the community, especially the under privileged. Working with the prisoners from North Sea Camp, and giving them the chance to start a new life, was a good example. But even more satisfying was helping people with learning difficulties. That was the route taken by the club's kit man, Jason Hatfield, now acknowledged as one of the best in the game.

It gives me a good feeling that I was able to help Jason fulfil his potential, which could so easily have remained hidden beneath his disability. I have been called Mr United, but that is a title which should be given to Jason who is now such a big part of everything around the club, and who has developed a social life, as well as a working routine, that could so easily have been denied him.

Jason, the grandson of United supporter, former Mayor of Boston, and Labour councillor for the Borough, the late Dennis Hatfield, was part of the BossCat group which encouraged those with a learning disability to take part in productive activities. They were based on the Marsh Lane industrial estate and, under supervision, made concrete items, and learned woodworking and

Long serving kitman Jason Hatfield

gardening skills. United would often purchase some of the items they had made to use as raffle prizes in the annual golf tournament.

Jason was keenly interested in football, and is a big supporter of Liverpool, and his supervisors asked if he could come to York Street to do odd jobs around the ground. Some of his friends came too, over the years, but it was Jason who emerged as the star pupil.

He started coming for just half a day a week, then that turned into a full day, then two days a week and, eventually, every day. He helped in so many different ways and became so very useful to the club, especially with the kit, helping to wash it and pack it. He was spending so much time at the club that BossCat decided that it would be a good idea if he became a full-time volunteer worker at the club. We were only too pleased to agree.

He became almost part of my family, was good friends of my daughters, and a popular and respected member of the BUFC extended family.

Jason's family became good friends and supporters of the club but, sadly, his lovely mum, Sandra Lovelace, died of breast cancer in 2008. This hit Jason very badly but, thanks to the new resilience he had found through working at the club, and the loving support of his family and friends, he battled on and continued to make progress.

Remember, he could not even make a cup of tea when he first came as a volunteer. Now he is regarded as a top-class kit man, and does many other jobs around the Jakemans Stadium. He goes to the bank, does the shopping, runs errands, helps at the golftournament, attends training and all matches, home and away.

Jason is one of the most important people around the club, and it gives me a great deal of pleasure to think that I was able to help him flourish, and one of the things that saddened me about retirement was having to leave people like Jason, and hoping that my successors would continue to look after him. I am sure that they will. I think Jason may have had some difficulty in coming to terms with my departure, and wondered who would take him to training etc, but that has now been resolved .

Boston United is now his life, but it has also been a passport to a wider circle of friends. He has a very supportive family and lives with his step-father Phil Lovelace, is close to step-brothers Billy and George , and spends weekends with his grandmother, Margaret Hatfield.

Jason has developed a taste for a pint or two of beer, and can often be seen in the company of another stalwart United supporter, Roy Hackford. The Coach and Horses, in Main Ridge, was one of his favourite haunts. He used to serve behind the bar there on occasions.

Nowadays he can be seen in the Pilgrim Lounge, the Eagle in West St reet, and, on most Friday evenings he and Roy enjoy a meal and a pint at the Castle, Haltoft End.

Working for Boston United has given me many opportunities to meet influential people, represent the club at important meetings, and serve on key committees, indeed do 101 things, but nothing gives me more pleasure than to reflect on the achievements of my friend, Jason Hatfield .

Characters I can call friends

Sid Blain has re-defined the meaning of Football Fanatic. It is doubtful that there is anyone else like him in the United Kingdom. If there is, I have not met him!

Although he lives in the Manchester area and watches Manchester City, his big love is non-League football. It is a toss up whether he loves football more than he loves food, but if the two go together then he is in seventh heaven. I am sure that it was the food, as well as the football, that attracted him to Boston.

I first met Sid more than 30 years ago when he was travelling all over the country as salesman for a shoe cleaning company. It was a job which went hand in hand with his hobby. Given the chance, Sid would watch football matches every day of the week, and it was even better if he could fit in two on one day.

His favourite team is Barrow, and a dream came to fruition when he was invited to join their

Long time friend Sid Blain

board of directors in September 2016, especially when he was given the task of looking after the catering in the boardroom!

He was one of the original "groundhoppers" - fans who would watch football anywhere in England, Wales and Scotland.

Maureen and I were invited to the wedding reception at Prestwich, Manchester, when he married Carol in July 1985 (out of season, you will note!). Vows were exchanged the day before. Maureen's sister Jackie was living at Frodsham, near Runcorn, at the time, so we were able also to visit her.

Long before it was sanctioned, Sid was a big advocate of Sunday football, and this was clear when United, anxious to complete their fixtures, had a double-header, playing at Lancaster on the Saturday and South Liverpool on the Sunday. The journey to Lancaster was in some of the heaviest snow I have ever seen - it was three feet deep in Barlborough-and we did not arrive until 4pm, being fined £8 by the Northern Premier League for causing a late kick-off. Because of the bad weather, we had been unable to pick up some of our players and I was substitute for both matches - but did not get a game and there was only one sub in those days!

After a goalless draw at Lancaster, we stayed overnight at the Euro Hotel near Runcorn, and ex-England and Liverpool star, Emlyn Hughes, was holding a testimonial event there. We were invited in and had our photographs taken with Emlyn. When we travelled to South Liverpool the next day, their pitch, at the old Holly Park ground, was under water but we still managed to complete the game and earned a point in another 0-0 draw. Guess who was on the terraces? Yes, the one and only Sid Blain, showing his support for Sunday football.

Incidentally, these were the only two NPL matches played that weekend.

Sid was also central to the drama when I organised a Sunday match at York St reet. Again he felt that it was his duty to be present to show his support for Sunday fo ot ball; and it was probably a good job that he w as.

About an hour before the scheduled kick-off a police inspector arrived determined, it seemed, to prevent us from playing because he said we were infringing Sunday trading law s. But he was no match for Sid, who soon became involved in the argument and advised us to put a discreet notice in the re-bate of the door to the directors' room saying that this was a FREE DOOR if anyone objected to paying for admission on a Sunday. Of course, none of the supporters knew it was there, but the Police officer admitted defeat in the face of Sid's ingenuity, and left the ground. Proudest man at York Street that day was Sid Blain .

In 1982 when we drew Sheffield United in the FA Cup, Sid was desperate to attend the match but, unfortunately, the directors' room and box, were so full that I was unable to squeeze him in either, and he had to sit in the stand and was unable to enjoy the directors' room hospitality. He moaned at me non-stop . I think it was because his stomach was suffering withdrawal symptons.

Whenever he visited Boston, Sid liked to stay at the New England Hotel, not only because it was near the ground but also because he loved their carvery! On the evening prior to that Sheffield United cup tie, Maureen and I met Sid to enjoy a meal from this very carvery, and his parting shot as we bid him goodnight was: "You had better be up early in the morning."

Well, of course I was up early ready to face a big day, but as I walked out of our house in Spilsby Road I noticed someone leaning on my car. It was Sid waiting for me. He was dressed in his running kit, and had been out for an early morning jog - and he was still moaning about being excluded from boardroom hospitality. Lincolnshire sausages were his big favourites, but he was going to miss them that day. Later, he developed a taste for cod bites from Eagles Fish Restau rant.

Over the years we have met on many occasions, in many different places, and even gone on an early morning run together before the Conference AGM. He is a true friend and complete football "nut". Early in my retirement days I received a telephone call from him, enquiring how I was. He was watching the Dafabet Welsh Premier League match between Gap Connahs Quay and Rhyl. He was keen to know how United had fared the day before at Altrincham, where his best friend, Andrew Shaw (another football fanatic) is a director.

Another person with whom I have maintained contact over the years is former top-class referee Peter Tyldsley, from Stockport. I met him many years ago when he refereed in the old Northern Premier League. He was in charge of the NPL Cup final when we lost to Matlock Town at Manchester City's Maine Road Ground, the day after our daughter Lisa was born on May 3rd 1978.

He has also been over to Boston to referee friendlies, and officiated at the NPL champions v SPL champions play-off. He still comes to seek me out when United play at Stockport.

When I think of characters I have known during my football years, one local man always comes to mind, and that is Michael Baxter, unfortunately no longer with us. Michael had a disability which required him to use two small walking sticks, but his lack of mobility did not stop him from being a fanatical Boston United supporter, ever present at home and away fixtures.

At York Street he could always be seen -and heard - near the old tunnel behind the goal. He was a familiar sight to all the players. Michael lived with his mother in Kirton and, despite his difficulties, he travelled the length and breadth of the country to follow the Pilgrims.

He overcame his handicap and learned to drive, his first vehicle being a small three-wheeled invalid car which took him, on his own, to wherever United were playing. When the long journeys took him to places like Weymouth or Bath, he would stay overnight on Friday with his brother in Oxford. On one occasion we were travelling home in the team coach along the A1, when we came across Michael, broken down, unable to move, and unable to contact anyone. There were no mobile 'phones in those days. Imagine how desperate he must have felt. We were able to come to the rescue of Michael, but not of his little three-wheeler. We lifted Michael onto the coach, but had to leave his car to be collected later. It was a moment when his dedication to Boston United really hit you, and how brave and determined he was not to allow his disability prevent him from enjoying his adventurous trips.

Later, his travels became more comfortable as he obtained a specially adapted car, and he rarely missed a match until, after moving with his mother to live at Butterwick, he became too infirm to attend games. Nevertheless, he still managed to ring the club office to find out the result whenever there was a match featuring his favourite team .It was a sad day when, after a short stay in a local nursing home, Michael passed away on March 29th 2016 at the age of 69. Emotions were running high when Chris Cook, Glen Madd ison and I represented Boston United at the funeral of one of its most dedicated supporters.

A very good friend over the years has been Peter Jones, Premier Division and European referee, who is now an assessor coach and EUFA assessor. Since my retirement he has telephoned regularly to check that I am OK. A terrific friend. We first met when he refereed United matches, and he was responsible for me having one of my most memorable days out in football. On a day when United were free of fixtures, he invited me to be his guest when he was refereeing a Tottenham Hotspurs vWatford FA Cup tie.

I went to Loughborough to travel with him by train to London, and by taxi to the ground. He took me into the dressing rooms and onto the pitch and introduced me to the Spurs secretary, and I had a front row seat ....and Spurs won 5-3. A terrific day out.

When he was officiating in Europe, he always brought home a gift for my friend Jason Hatfield, something from Real Madrid or Barcelona for instance. The fact that he has been great with Jason shows the nature of the man. He was a surprise visitor to my 65th birthday and to my testimonial match and his friendship means a great deal to me.

Another long friendship I cherish is with the BBC's favourite Match of the Day commentator John Matson who, of course, had relatives in Bost on.

At Tower Road School I was in the same class as his cousin Jayne Matson who lived opposite the school. John used to visit his late uncle in Boston and was often accompanied by his father, a former Methodist Minister at Sw in eshead. Another of his relatives worked for J Carr and Sons in Bost on, when I worked for my dad.

I met John for the first time when he came to a function in town, and I also met him when United played away to Barnet , where he started his journalistic career on the local new spaper. John was an avid football programme collector and I sent him a programme from every Boston United match. Over the years we also became friendly with John's wife, Ann, and son Frederick. When our daughter Lisa was in Great Ormond Street Hospital, John visited her with a card signed by Gary Lineker and Paul Gascoigne.

We still keep in touch, exchange Christmas cards, and occasional telephone calls, and whenever he visits Boston he usually calls to see me.

Peter Jones invited me and Jason to a Sportsman's Dinner at Leicester City when

John was the guest spea ker. We surprised John when he was chatting with ex-Leicester star, Alan Burchinal!.

One man who seems to have been around York Street forever is Des Portas. If you don't recognise his face, you will remember his voice because he was the man behind the mike tracking United's performances for Radio Lincolnshire over many years. He was famous for his meticulous preparation for his match reports, and for the records and statistics he has maintained on the club.

Now retired from his job as a BT engineer, Des is an authority on the club. He has been - and still is - a fanatical supporter of The Pil grims. I gather that he has dedicated one bedroom at his home in Willoughby Road to a huge collection of newspapers, books, magazines and cuttings mainly relating to Boston United.

In his younger days he was a hard working member of the old supporters' club, and I recall, in my early time with United, he and Danny Pettigrew ran round the perimeter of the pitch to raise funds for the club.

Des joined Pilgrim Radio when they started broadcasting United matches, both home and away, for the benefit of patients at Pilgrim Hospital. He made such a good job of it that he was invited to do a similar thing for Radio Lincolnshire. He has often been called upon to be MC for various other events in the area, particularly boxing tournament s.

If you don't recognise Des by his face or voice, then you may identify him as the man with a baseball cap, adorned by many club metal badges, busy organising charity collections at the ground. Nowadays he is a big supporter of the Royal British Legion and is a prominent collector for the Poppy Day Appeal, and is also a keen supporter of the Royal Society for the Protection of Birds.

Although his broadcasting days are over, Des is a season ticket holder on the Spayne Road terrace at York Street where his wife Pat, in her more mobile days, was a long-standing supporter usually found behind the York Street goal.

Their son, James and grandson Travis, also have United connections. James, as a young lad, regularly accompanied his dad to matches, and now helps out with ground maintenance, Travis has played in goal for the youth side . Yes, Des and his family have been big supporters of Boston United and it is difficult to imagine York Street without him being around.

Another familiar voice at the ground is that of matchday announcer Mick Fixter, who I have known since our schooldays. Mick followed Nick Thompson into the announcer's box. Nick had joined the Gliderdrome staff from leaving school and, a fanatical supporter, he has tackled so many tasks such as helping with the lotteries, painting around the ground, you name it, Nick is likely to have done it. He was an invaluable member of the club.

His late wife, worked in the club office, and their daughter Becky was brought up in the club family. When the Malkinson family distanced themselves from the day to day running of the club, so did Nick and his place as matchday announcer was taken by Mick Fixter, a fanatical supporter as well as being a follower of speedway and lover of music. He rarely misses a game, at home or away, and, on my retirement, was still going strong. Let's hope that will continue for many years, with his assistant, Russell Howard, stepping in when required. Russell travels all the way from Louth to help out.

In the case of an emergency, Des Portas has been called in to help out as announcer, as has his prodigy, journalist Scott Dalton well-known for his Radio Lincolnshire reports on United matches and other activities, and now holding the prestigious position of presenter of the breakfast programme at the radio station.

One highly respected local family who have had three generations of involvement with Boston United have been the Blades, starting with Jack and Lily, a popular husband and wife team who enhanced the club's reputation of giving a warm welcome to the boardroom to guests and visiting officials.

They were in situ when I first joined the club. Jack, heavily involved in local sport, had a key role with Lincolnshire Tractors who were based at Kirton, and was always available to help out where he could with United, especially in the field of publicity.

On match days he and Lily, a lady with a lovely, friendly smile, were hosts in the boardroom and, well aware of the importance of public relations, Jack never failed to make the tricky journey from the directors' room up the stairs to the Press Box precariously carrying a tray full of cups of tea-and rarely spilling a drop.

Jack and Lily had three children, Derek, Wendy and Maureen. Wendy, who became Mrs Eanor, was a star table tennis player, but it was Maureen who continued the link with thePilgrims- by marrying one of the players from the era of all that Derby County and Tottenham Hotspur FA Cup excitement. Geoff Snade was the highly-rated left back in that team of legends.

He previously played for Chesterfield but came to live in Boston when signed by Ray Middleton, and has made his home in the town ever sinc e. He can still be seen at United home matches, no doubt reflecting on the days when he was involved in those historic matches of previous years.

His father-in-law Jack also ran another local business, Thomas Mineral Waters,

130

which was based in Bargate End, and Geoff worked there until, I believe, it closed. When Jack and Lily retired from their boardroom duties, Maureen took over and, luckily for the club, is still there as the friendly face to welcome guests.

Geoff and Maureen had two children, Russell and Nicolette, and it was Nicci who maintained the family tradition of being involved with the club when, on leaving school, she worked in the office helping me on the commercial side of things, alongside Sue Barwick and Linda Thompson.

Nicci married Kitwood Boys and Haven High school teacher, Colin Woodcock, and the relationship with United continued with Colin, a friend ofthe Malkinson family, becoming a director and, later, easing my workload by becoming company secretary.

Colin, who had the reputation of being a good snooker player and golfer, played a major role alongside David Monks, Pat and Andrew Malkinson, and me, in establishing the annual Boston United Golf Tournament at Boston Golf Club as one of the best such events in the county, attracting almost 50 teams and offering a vast array of prizes. Of course organising such an event required lots of meetings, usually held at the Cowbridge Inn, involving a beer or two - or more. And sometimes a ticking off from the wives!

These are just some of the people who have helped match days to "tick", and who have been so important to the smooth-running of the club.

Another, and one of the most popular, is the club Chaplain, Canon the Rev John Moore, one of the nicest people I have ever met. John went into the church after first experiencing life in industry, and starting his new calling in the Grimsby area before becoming Vicar of St Thomas' Church in Boston.

This appointment involved visits to St Thomas Primary School where he thought a good project for the pupils would be for them to interview Boston United players, past and present. I would hate to suggest that a clergyman of John Moore's standing would have an ulterior motive, but I can 't help thinking that the initiative came about because he was a long-standing United supporter who would get as much enjoyment out of talking to the players as would the pupils.

Anyway, I remember him coming to me to seek contact details, and I was happy to oblige. Subsequently the children produced articles for the matchday programme, and for the Target new spaper . Good experience, and a sense of achievement for them, and an enjoyable project for John.

From this beginning, Canon Moore became more involved with the club he had supported since being a boy, helping out in various ways, until he was invited to become the club's Chaplain. In this role, which continues to the present, he has become a good friend, and big help, to officials, players and supporters alike, and has become a very important person at the club. Never afraid to help out in any capacity, he has given a hand in the boardroom, taken players and kit to away matches in his own car, and is always welcomed warmly at other clubs.

When he moved to Coningsby, where he also looked after Tattershall and another parish, he still found time for United's home and away matches.

Our younger daughter Katie was never christened as a baby but, at the age of 23, decided that it was time she ought to be, and the Rev John came to the rescue. He adds his own personal touch to such events and conducted a lovely Service of Baptism for Katie at the historic Holy Trinity Church, Tattershall. It was a special occasion the like of which she would never have remembered had she been a baby.

Over the years, Canon Moore has become known as something of a "funeral specialist" and has offered comfort, support and solace to many people suffering the trauma following the bereavement of loved ones. I, among many others, was helped by the comforting services which he conducted at the funerals of my father, mother and mother-in-law. Now retired, and living in the East Lincolnshire village of Huttoft, his is still a welcome presence around York Street. Long may it continue.

In search of money

One thing football clubs always want is money. As much as possible. They have an insatiable thirst for it-and never-ending ideas on how to spend it. Money has been behind United's major successes; and the lack of it has brought the times of crisis .

I was thrown into the deep end of fundraising when I first stepped in to help the club when secretary Ray Middleton was taken ill. I soon found that it was one of the biggest and most important jobs at the club.

Fireside Bingo was the name of the game at the time. The crimped-edged tickets were sold at 5p a time all around Lincolnshire, Cambridgeshire, Norfolk, Nottinghamshire, Leicestershire and Derbyshire, and was one of the most successful fundraisers in the region.

We had a team of girls sorting and packing the tickets to send out to the public, and some of the names that come to mind are Sue Burton, Sue Barwick, Cheryl Beasley, Judy Edwards, Linda Thompson and Angela Lewis.

I don't know whose brainchild the fundraising ideas were, but it is maybe no coincidence that the Malkinson family, with years of experience in the entertainments industry, had an uncanny knack of knowing what would appeal to the public.

After the bingo tickets came the Pilgrim Lottery, and United were the first semi-professional club to launch this type of competition, with a £1,000 first prize, a lot of money for the time . We were following in the footsteps of Football League trendsetters Notts County and Plymouth Argyle.

We changed just as the lottery laws changed, and we came under the jurisdiction of the Gaming Board. The new competition was a big hit . I was going out four days a week seeking agents and delivering tickets. Norfolk, Cambridgeshire and Lincolnshire were the most popular areas . We also started selling scratch cards with a £1,000 first prize.

The Pilgrim Lottery draw became a big event in its own right. It was held every Monday evening in the Pilgrim Lounge, in those days called the Social Clu b. It attracted a lot of people and it became a special evening, so much so that we decided to take it on tour to our customers from further afield. We had a lot of followers who liked to go to every draw, wherever in the county it was being held. If, for instance, the chosen venue was in Skegness, it was nothing unusual to take two coach loads from Boston.

In addition to the £1,000 first prize, there was £500 for second, and £200 for third, plus a mystery prize and many other smaller prizes, all chosen via a Random Number Selector. My round usually started at about 8-30am, and I arrived back in Boston at about 5-30pm, having, on a Monday, visited places like Spalding, Holbeach, Long Sutton, King's Lynn and Wisbech where we had a lady called Maureen Grainger who looked after all the agents in that area.

My wife Maureen also had a round in the county, selling tickets and collecting money. Her yellow van was a well-known sight on the Lincolnshire roads. When our daughter Lisa was born, Maureen would take her along and, on a Thursday, she would arrive in Horncastle at about lunch time and go to Danby's shop for food, and also take the opportunity to feed Lisa and change her nappy.

Another person Maureen visited in Horncastle was Miss Moorhouse who provided lodgings for Irish farmworker s. A lasting memory was of the big pots on the cooker as she prepared their evening meal. Another stop-off was at gents hairdresser, Ron Short. We also had an agent in Aston, Sheffield - Mr Burge-who would sell about 2,000 scratch-off tickets every fortnight. He also had a caravan at Chapel St Leonards and would sell the tickets to holidaymakers around the caravan parks. Bostonian Barry Pearson had general stores in Skegness and Chapel St Leonards and he would also sell a lot of tickets.

In the heyday of the lotteries it was nothing to sell 10,000 tickets a week. It was handy that our offices in Spain Place were opposite The Gliderdrome which attracted big crowds to their bingo nights, and the punters there often called in to buy lottery tickets as we were open from 6 to 9-30pm to catch their trade.

It was the success of the Lottery which enabled the York Street ground to be re-developed in 1978 after the disappointment of it being rejected as not being up to Football League standard when United had won the right to be considered for election to the League. That was the year that Wigan Athletic, runners-up to United in the Northern Premier League, were voted into the League.

After the success of the Pilgrim Lottery, we moved on to the Alphabetical Forecast, another good money spinner, but the days of such competitions came to an end with the arrival of the National Lottery. We could not compete with a draw that was destined to make people millionaires overnight.

Another feature of life with Boston United was the Social Club, a hive of entertainment which, from a Nissan hut in a grass field, emerged into a very busy venue. It was home to darts, pool, dominoes, football and quiz teams, as well as live entertainment which saw the club packed with 200 people on Saturday and Sunday evenings.

Full-time stewards included Eric and Marion Baines . Eric was a Bostonian who was in the Navy, stationed at Weymouth, but gave up his job to take over at the club with his wife.

Success at the club continued under the stewardship of local licensees Joyce and Vernon Greenhough, Graham and Donna Late, and David Munks.

It was my job to book the entertainment and I remember when I arranged for ladies mud wrestling to take place at the club, we had a packed house and took £550 at the bar. Trouble was that there was mud everywhere and it took a lot of cleaning up afterwards, but that did not stop local lads wanting to take on the female wrestlers in the ring .

I recall Steve Elsam, whose wife Beverley worked in the club offices, decided to be one of the volunteer wrestl ers. He was keen that we should not tell Beverley , but she found out and he was in big trouble! After the bouts, the wrestlers used the dressing rooms at the football ground to clean up, all in the bath together, ladies and men!

Boston United's social club, now known as The Pilgrim Lounge
since it's refurbishment by Chestnut Homes in 2006

Inspecting other clubs' grounds

I was thrilled to be invited to serve on the management committee of the Football Confe rence. It was a first for Boston United and I felt that it was an honour for both me and the club- although not everyone agreed. Chairman Mr Ernest Malkinson, for instance, thought it would take up too much of my time-time that was needed by the club. However, I accepted the invitation put to me by Conference chairman, Jim Thompson, at the annual meeting in Blackpool, and I served for nine years until United left the competition, and I was invited to serve on the Northern Premier League management committee which I did for five years.

Meetings were mostly on a Thursday, at the Cafe Royal, London, and it was in an era when bomb scares were not unusual. On one occasion there were explosions in the area and we were shepherded into the basement of the hotel until it was declared safe to leave to catch our trains. A frightening experience.

I attended disciplinary meetings, and travelled all over the country as a member of the Ground Grading Committee which was called to inspect grounds of clubs that were poised for promotion to the Conference . There were some interesting expeditions. One was to Fisher Athletic in the docks area of London. The inspection committee that day was made up of Peter Hunter (Conference secretary), Cyril Gingell (Kettering Town) and me. We were met by ...well, there was a pitch, but little else. Just empt iness. No t erraces. No toilet s. Very little fencing round the pitch.

I can find no other words to describe the club's representatives than a group of heavies, and they did not hide their displeasure when we told them their ground had failed the inspection. There was more than a veiled threat of what might happen to us if we did not approve the ground on a second inspection two weeks later. It was not a little frightening.

For this second visit we were joined by Ken Marsden, Chairman of the Northern Premier League, and a representative of the Isthmian League. There to greet us were the same club officials and, surprise, surprise, everything we had asked for on the previous visit had been completed , and there was no difficulty in passing the ground as being fit for the Conference. We did not need the biggest, tastiest buffet I have ever seen to help us make our decision, but enjoyed it all the same .

We had a wasted journey when we went to inspect The Crabble at Dover, the same three who had visited Fisher Athletic. On this occasion there was nothing to inspect, only a large crane standing on the centre circle ready to put steelwork up around the terraces. There was no sign of the steelwork. It wasn't a difficult decision to fail the ground. On a second visit, with other representatives of feeder league clubs, all the steelwork was up, and the ground was almost ready for football. This time it was an easy decision to grant "a pass".

The weather was terrible when we inspected two grounds on one day, and it was a long journey for me, setting out at 6am, to Hyde United and Colne Dynamoes. At Hyde we found a plastic pitch standing in water and dressing rooms located in a nearby school. We gave advice on what improvements were needed, and then set out for Colne up in the hills near Blackburn. It had not stopped raining for 24 hours.

They were running away with the Northern Premier League at the time, with a team of full-time players. Perhaps it was because their pitch had one of the worst slopes I had ever seen. It was flooded on the occasion of our visit. Everything around the ground was made with plywood. The club owner was involved in the timber industry. The ground failed the inspection.

I left Colne at 6pm, and that was the start of the nightmare. I did not arrive home until 3am the next day. The weather was appalling and there was carnage on the roads almost all the way home ....upturned lorries, buildings demolished, roads flooded, you name it.

One ground inspection I will always remember was at Stalybridge Celtic who were seeking to join the Conference from the NPL. After lunching in their Social Club with secretary Martin Torr and chairman Peter Barnes, we walked around the ground. My colleagues wanted to turn it down because of the old wooden stand, but I disagreed and suggested ways in which the ground could be brought up to standard. They agreed to do the work and eventually passed the inspection.

Subsequently when I have visited matches at Stalybridge they have thanked me in their matchday programme for the suggestions I made that day. They now have a first-class stand and ground, and say that my suggestions helped them on their way.

One other management committee I was on when I was younger, much younger, was that of Boston and District Football League .

Maureen my biggest supporter

Readers will have noticed - or at least I hope they have - that Maureen has been mentioned frequently in MY story. She has, in fact, been my biggest supporter and ally in our 43 years of marriage and has played a key role in the Boston United family. My story is her story too. She is still working at the club, with more responsibility since my retirement, and is enjoying being there as much as ever.

Our two daughters will tell you that their growing up has been squeezed into the time allowed by our commitment to the club. Nevertheless, they have grown into fine young ladies who have made us very proud.

Maureen's first involvement with the club was when Jim Smith was player-manager, and just after the birth of our first daughter, Lisa, when Jim asked her if she would help his wife Yvonne to run the snack bar in the old wooden building on the Spayne Road terraces. She agreed and her involvement at the club has carried on to this very day.

When the Smiths left on Jim's appointment as manager of Colchester, Maureen continued running the snack bar with the help of her mother, Mrs Mitcham, Julie Pawson, Sarah and Samantha Scrupps, with me being co-opted as the errand boy fetching food, drinks, sweets, crisps, pies etc from Cash and Carry.

Maureen also prepared all the food for players, directors and sponsors in those days and our daughters will remind you, if I don't, that Christmas Day celebrations in the Blackwell household were often cut short as we had to prepare the food ready to take to the ground the following day for the Boxing Day match. After years as an ever-present in the snack bar, Maureen began helping out with the lottery rounds and combined this with a new role serving-with Ray Parker- refreshments in the new vice-presidents' room under the York Street stand.

When United gained promotion to the Football League, and the workload increased with the extra demands, she worked full-time in the office as receptionist, ticket office administrator, and Disabled Officer. She is still working there, popular with staff and supporters.

Lisa also became involved early in her working life when she helped out at the new Study Support Office alongside Jan Mclucas. BUFC was the first non-League club to be involved in this scheme to work with local schoolchildren. Initially, they worked from an office in the old Christians' transport building, next to The Gliderdrome, before moving to the Cropleys VP lounge at the ground.

More staff joined as it became an important part of the club's activities, and Lisa worked as a teacher under the direction of Oognah Quinn after Jan Mclucas left. Sadly, the funding ended for this popular project, and everyone involved was made redundant.

During the time that Jim Rodwell was Chief Executive, our younger daughter Katie was involved on matchdays, helping to count the gate money.

All the family have spent many hours at the club and, on reflection, it could be argued that we were too obsessive, and the girls will say that we put football and BUFC before them. All I can say is that, as much as Maureen and I have enjoyed working for the football club, our love for the girls has always been much greater .
I have been known to be emotional on occasions, and this has never been more evident than at my final home game as General Manager, against Nuneaton, on April 23rd 2016.

It wasn't just the realisat ion that the parting of the ways had finally arrived between John Blackwell and Boston United that brought tears to my eyes, but the article that Lisa had written in the matchday programme, was particularly heart-warming ... and heart-wrenching.

It would be remiss of me if I did not print it here. This is what she wrote:

"I am nearly 38 years old now and, for as long as I can remember, my dad has been at Boston United. My whole family's life has revolved around the club.

"I grew up thinking dad was famous. He was always in the newspapers and on the radio, and everyone knew him. Wherever we are he gets stopped, and ends up talking to someone he knows.

"When my sister and I were growing up, we were always there following both our mum and dad around, either at the ground or the office in Spain Place.

"I spent a lot of time with dad. I would go out with him when he did the lottery ticket round, if he had to go and meet players, or on every day errands. I also went to Wembley in 1985 on the bus following the players, and I even worked at the Study Support Centre.

"Dad would spend every day and every moment at the cluB .....even on Christmas Day he would open a few presents with us and then go to check the ground!

"We never really had a holiday as a whole family. Dad would go for days out, but would always want to get back for w ork . It felt like he was on call all hours of the day, not through duty, but through his own choice.

"I have never known anyone with so much passion, dedication and loyalty, and he has put his heart and soul into Boston United.

"I have seen all the highs and heartache Dad has dealt with throughout his time with the club. I know he must be a ve,y strong person, but he just loved his job .

"All this time I have moaned about not having him fully there, that he was always at work and it felt like we *came second to the club, now I can't imagine him not being there. It was what he lived for, and I don't know what he is going to do now without it. "He said he's going to write a book . While at the club he has made a lot of friends, and he's got lots of stories and tales to tell. It is a good job that he has got a ve,y good memory.*

"I didn't realise what he meant to everyone, but hearing what people have said about him has made me see that he was appreciated and recognised for his lifelong dedication to the Pilgrims.

"The club won't be the same without him. He will always be remembered as Mr Boston United, and I am so proud that he is my dad."

Well, there you have it, from someone who know s. What more can I say?

Games I missed

Perhaps I should not have been so conscientious, perhaps I should have put family before football more often than I did. I am sure that Maureen and our two daughters must have thought so at times but, right or wrong, I am proud of the fact that I only missed four of United's games during the 38 years I worked for the club. That means, I have estimated, that I attended more than 1,200 matches, home and away. I can recall the four that I missed:

1 The home game against Nuneaton Borough when daughter Lisa was undergoing life-saving heart surgery in Great Ormond Street Hospital.

2 A game at Runcorn because it clashed with an international match being played at York Street, and I had to stay behind to make sure arrangements ran smoothly.

3 and 4 Fisher Athletic v Boston United on two occasions. I had to stay behind to organise our Tote draw on the Monday night. Keeping the money coming into the club through the popular fundraiser was more important than attending a football match.

The international match was for the English Schools FA at under 15 level for the Victory Shield between England and Wales on February 20th 1988. It was a massive compliment, and honour, to the club that we had been asked to organise such a prestigious event which attracted an attendance of more than 3,500. I was honoured by an invitation to lead the Welsh team onto the pitch.

It took almost a year to complete the arrangements, with schools travelling from all over the country. Providing parking for coaches was one of the headaches. But there was also the booking of hotel rooms for both teams, arranging a banquet at the New England Hotel, the presentation of medals and caps afterwards in the Social Club, all the culmination of a series of meetings with England Schools FA officials, Pat Smith (national) and Rod Dunn (local). I also arranged all sponsorship of this match.

Two other important fixtures I arranged at York Street also involved the English Schools FA when their representative teams played against sides selected by the Football Association. This was in the days when the English Schools FA held their massive annual tournament in Lincolnshire, based at the Derbyshire Miners Welfare Centre in Skegness. This lasted all week and county teams played each other on grounds all round the county. There were scouts at pretty well every game to run the rule over so much talent.

When the representative matches were played at York Street, all these players were brought into Boston to support those who had been selected to play in the game which was the highlight of the tournament.

I remember Trevor Brooking (West Ham and England) and Alan Gowling (Manchester United) playing in one of these mat ches. Former Boston Grammar School boy, and ex-United player, Mick Lyons, represented England Schools in one fixture .

The Community Shield match at under 18 level, England v Wales, was played at York Street on March 5th 2009.

Since I retired, and had accepted the role as club President, I have missed games, the first one being a pre-season friendly at Gateshead on the last Saturday before the season started on August 6th 2016, and the league fixture away to Gloucester City (played at Cheltenham) when I really didn't have any excuse for not going out with the family on a Bank Holiday.

But old habits die hard, and I kept in touch with how the match was going by telephone.

Escort was a bank robber

As soon as we stepped into the bank, Barclays branch in Boston's Market Place, my companion, Mick, started laughing . Something had certainly touched his sense of humour. I soon found out what it was. "The last time I was in a bank, I was standing on the counter with a shotgun demanding money," he chuckled.

Bizarrely, I knew he was a bank robber when I asked him to escort me with United gate money, plus cash from fundraising. I can't remember how much we were banking that day, but it would be a sizeable amount . And I knew that he had had a lifetime of crime. On reflection, it was, perhaps, taking temptation a bit far. Strangely, I never gave his past history a thought that day. I trusted him, just as I trusted other prisoners over the years. I found that most of them responded to trust.

Mickey the Fish - working hard, but I don't think the game went ahead!

Mick was one of the most notorious inmates at our local open prison, North Sea Camp, and was well into his 15-year sentence for that bank raid when he joined us at Boston United to do odd jobs around the ground as a step towards his rehabilitation. He was a Brummie and had been in and out of prison all his life. Stories he told about his past would make your hair curl.

Despite his unpromising cv, he turned out to be a model worker, fitted in well to life at the football club, became a very good friend to my wife and myself, and got on well with everyone around the club - and even became a regular visitor to the home of chairman, Pat Malkinson, for Sunday lunch .

Well, actually, it was Sunday lunch held on Mondays because weekend commitments at the Gliderdrome for the Malkinson family meant Sundays were too busy for the traditional meal. This was just one example of the non-judgemental, and generous, attitude of Pat and his wife Pauline, who simply saw any prisoners working at the club as part of the greater family, and they loved having their family round for Monday's Sunday lunch .

Mick was the second prisoner to come to work for us. The part we played in the rehabilitation scheme came about through Paul Hocking, father of former United player Matt. Paul -well-known in local sporting circles himself at the time-was an officer at the Category C prison.

The Governor and his staff were looking for organisations willing to give prisoners the chance to work in the community as preparation for the time when they were released from prison. After numerous meetings with Paul and fellow officers, it was agreed that United would become part of the scheme and the first to join us was a Leicester lad, David, who was cutting grass in Freiston churchyard when we met for the first time.

After that tentative start, BUFC and NSC became partners in a big way, with useful benefits to both parties. Our part of the bargain was to provide gainful employment, and a hot midday meal, which we organised with theCosy Cafe , next to the snooker hall in Artiilery Way.

David's stay with us was a mutual success, and he keeps in touch to this very day with a Christmas card and a 'phone call now and again. It was when David was released that bank robber Mick was introduced to us. NSC officers felt that, despite his forbidding past record, he deserved the chance to work in the community, and we agreed to give him that chance. Again it worked out well, and Mick was with us for a long time, sometimes working alongside other prisoners, all of whom enjoyed the chair man 's hospitality on Mondays.

It was while Mick was with us, that the North Sea Camp soccer team, members of the Boston Football League, reached the final of a local cup competition to be played at York Street in an evening match. For Mick, this was a big challenge. He wanted everything to be spick and span for the visit of HIS team. He could not have worked more diligently had Manchester United been the visit ors. Pitch and dressing rooms were immaculate.

The NSC Governor decided to allow all the inmates to attend the match, and coaches were hired to bring them to town, and the ground was packed with supporters in prison garb of blue duffle coats. It was an unbelievable occasion - a whole prison allowed out to watch a football match - and wives, girlfriends and relatives also turning out in force to take the opportunity of an unscheduled visit.

I don't think that too many of them were disappointed that their team   lost. Certainly the players weren't because, as their supporters were taken back to camp, they were allowed to celebrate their defeat in the Social Club. I have often wondered what Home Office rule allowed t hat. The soccer-playing prisoners were not bothered about whether the concession was covered by any Prison Governor's manual, and nor was Mick as he was allowed to stay and celebrate with them. The next morning when he came into work, he made for the physio's table and stayed there all day!

When Mick eventually left the prison, he became a regular visitor to York Street, and even attended Andrew Malkinson's wedding to Paula Carter, and the reception at The Gliderdrome.

After a while, there were no more visits from Mick. Apparently he had gone to live in Spain. I still smile at his nickname ... Mickey the Fish.

Following Mick into York Street was one of his pals, another Brummie, Jasper, who had been no stranger to prison life over the years. He was another real character who must have enjoyed his time with us because he still keeps in touch.

Another bank robber followed, but Claude was a smart young Londoner with a lovely wife and family who often visited him at the ground. Working with him was an older gentleman, Roy, from Hertfordshire, who was serving his first prison sentence after becoming involved in a scam stealing old metal from his workplace at British Aerospace in Hatfield.

During lunch breaks they would stand outside the ground eyeing up the young girls making their way to and from Boston College, and Claude used his good looks and charm to become friendly with one of them. She featured in his flamboyant release from NSC. Apparently it is tradition for London prisoners - or at least some of them with the right connections - to be collected from the prison gates in a chauffeur-driven white Rolls Royce with champagne on board. And so it was for Claude.

On the way into Boston he collected his local girl friend as he came to say cheerio to all of us at York Street, the sight of the flash limousine causing a stir among neighbours and passers- by. A few years later Claude returned to Boston , having left his wife and family, to live with his ex-Boston College girl friend. They are no longer together, but he still lives in Boston, alone. He is well-known and well-liked in the town. Roy kept in touch for a while, but I have not heard from him for some time now.

The co-operation between BUFC and NSC continued for 15 years, and we hit the national Press on occasions. Ex-police officer Danny made the headlines when he cut the York Street pitch in waves. Unfortunately he was in the news again when he returned to crime after release from prison, reverting to his old habit of holding up banks and building societies.

I recall being visited by detectives from Nottingham who were investigating robberies in that area. They showed me photographs and, yes, I could recognise the culprit. It was Danny. He was eventually arrested while in a gym in Yorkshire, and received another ten-year sentence. Our rehabilitation efforts did not always work, it seems.

On one occasion we had a purge to smarten up the stadium. That involved painting pretty well everything that did not move, and all the work was done by prisoners. Fifteen were working at any one time; lots of interesting stories and lots of lunches to provide.

I don't know whether there is some kind of theme here, but there seemed to be a lot of Davids at North Sea Camp. Two come to mind. One was a top man, a good worker, took a keen interest in the club, and was liked by everyone. He still comes to see us and now drives a car transporter for a living.

Another David was a Lincolnshire man who got himself into trouble by trying to sort out somebody else's pub row. Unfortunately, he had a glass in his hand at the time, and was sent to prison for four years. He was a fencing contractor, a great worker who could turn his hand to anything. He started his prison life at Lincoln which proved a bit embarrassing for the authorities as he knew many of the prison officers; in fact, he had done work for a lot of them, so he had to be moved on. This David was a keen fisherman, and very successful in competitions. He still comes to see me and re-laid my drive and patio with block paving, as well as erecting a new fence. He used to call me Golden Goal because of the tickets I sold on match days.

Big Pete was a body builder from Kettering who used to keep in shape by running round the pitch, with a sack of coal strapped to his back, every lunch time. At a NSC sports day, he earned his place in the Guinness Book of Records by setting a new distance for carrying a bag of coal. On release from prison, Big Pete returned to this area to live with a local lady.

Back in the days when John Drewnicki was a director and Peter Morris was manager, we hit upon the idea of turning a space under the York Street stand into a vice-President's room. The area was at the end of turnstiles 3 and 4, and was our rubbish tip. John arranged for a delivery of bricks from London Brick Company in Peterborough, and NSC found two bricklayers to start the work.

One was a pigeon fancier who became friendly with a local man who shared his interest in the sport. They chatted, swapped ideas, and eventually exchanged pigeons, the inmate's wife bringing some to Boston and taking others home. One weekend the man disappeared. The pigeons came back, but he never did. After months on the run, he was found in the Leeds area.

146

Eventually, however, the new lounge was completed, thanks also to a supporter who was a builder, and who put in the drains, floor and windows. Years later the room was extended to become the Study Support Centre which was attended by local children. This was another great initiative by the football club, and our daughter Lisa worked there alongside Jan Mclucas and Oonagh Quinn among others. Eventually the scheme came to an end because of a change of policy by the Education Authority but, over the years, it had been of immense value to the United and, I believe, the many inmates who worked with us.

After a long break, the club received a letter from a footballing ex-inmate at NSC seeking a chance to play for the club. He had been at Birmingham City when Jim Smith was manager there. The new regime of David Newton and Neil Kempster agreed that he should be given a chance, provided that he worked at the ground.

Rob Wesley was substitute on a number of occasions, and finally played towards the end of the season before being released. I have not heard from him lately, but his mother was extremely grateful that we gave him the opportunit y.

As an addendum to our involvement with prisoners, there is a more recent story about a man called Chris, a one-time colleague of ex-policeman Graham Bean, the man who first visited the club when investigating breaches of FA regulations. Graham, who now runs Football Factors, has become a good friend, and he wrote to see if we could find a role for a former police officer who was in prison at Ranby and was due to move to North Sea Camp.

The chairman agreed that Chris could come to work on the ground, and, like many prisoners before him, he became a great asset to the club. One of his jobs was to paint yellow lines around the terraces. His wife was a serving sergeant in the Police Force and, on his release from prison, they both became supporters of Boston United, and could be seen at both home and away matches in recent times.

Getting used to retirement

July 6th 2016 was a strange day for me. United were due to learn of their fixtures for the coming season . It would be the first time in 38 years that I was not sitting in the office waiting to be the first person in the club to set eyes on the schedule for the new campaign. It had always been an occasion awaited with a tinge of excitement whatever league we were in and, of course, especially the debut season in League Two. I learned later that day what the 2016-17 fixtures would be when assistant manager Martyn Bunce called round to see me.

It all sounds so trivial now, but I was not finding retirement easy. Just 36 days had passed since I had left the club and I was still an apprentice retiree. Although I had announced on September 15th (my 68th birthday) the year before that I was stepping down as general manager-secretary at the end of the season, I was not prepared for the sudden change in lifestyle.

Football, and especially Boston United, was in my blood and, now I was alone at home, the 'phone, previously my constantly noisy companion, was silent. I didn't know what to do with myself. I knew, deep down, with the club on the verge of a new era and the move to a new stadium, it was time for me to leave. New skills were needed and everything was computer orientated and, no doubt, would be even more so in the future. I was a dinosaur in the fast-moving world of technolo gy.

The club was in good hands, led by David Newton and Neil Kempster, had a new Chief Executive in Mike Hardy, and Craig Singleton, a talented young man who should probably already have moved up the administrative ladder, was taking over the secretarial duties, as well as continuing with his commercial and media duties. And yet ... I am sure that I am not the first man - nor will be the last - to worry about seeing the job you have loved in someone else's hands. My last day at work was May 31st 2016.

On the day I announced my forthcoming retirement, September 1st 2015 after 38 years working for the club. I allowed my head to rule my heart. My heart was telling me that, although I was 68 and long past the age when most people would already have retired, I was fit enough to continue the job I had enjoyed so much, and had the kind of experience that no-one else in the club had. The contacts I had fostered would be lost.

My head was giving a conflicting message. There were changes afoot, big changes. A new ground was on the horizon, scheduled to be ready by 2018, we had been told . The new ground meant new facilities, new computerised systems. I was an old fashioned type of football administrator, pen, pencil and telephone being my tools, aided by personal contacts developed over the years. I did not want to hide behind a keyboard and screen, communicating with anonymous e-mails.

In fact, I had never used a computer, although I had a bit of training. I could have re-trained in the various skills which it is visualised will be necessary in the future. I had talked it through with the owners but, although they offered alternatives to retirement, I decided it was time to go.

The last day was a strange one. I had passed over all the information I thought would be useful to my successors. Only people at work were the new Chief Executive, Jason Hatfield, Martyn Bunce and my wife Maureen. My daughter had baked cakes for the staff. I think Jason ate most of them. I handed in my keys and, just before I left, vice-chairman, Neil Kempster dropped in to say thank you for all the work I had done, and to wish me well. I appreciated that. Then I just drove away. The end of a fantastic experience .

The next day I rose, as normal, at 6-15am, went to fetch my newspaper, had my breakfast, Maureen went to work. What was I doing to do? Wash up, a bit of housework, watch television. What else? Nothing came to mind.

I felt lonely and fed up for days, and then I was reminded that several people had suggested I should write a book. Might sound a good isea in theory, but how did I set about it? I had many boxes of cuttings and photographs stashed away, and George Wheatman, former Editor of both the Boston Standard (where he had also been Sports Editor), and the Boston Target, had also mentioned the idea on a few occasions in his Target column.

Coincidentally, his wife had also called into my office to request my telephone numbers. Perhaps she thought he could use his retirement more productively. Anyway, I made the call and arranged a meeting. After an interesting hour or two we made the decision to give it a go, and I believe that our regular meetings have been therapeutic for both of us. Certainly they have brought back lots of memories, and set me on track for a new life. The day before the new fixtures for 2016-17 were announced I had already passed my first difficult test. I am sure that many people will say that I was worrying too much. I was now President of the club, and it was an honour to be given that role, but if I showed too much interest would that be deemed as interfering, as failure to let go?

United were having their first pre-season practice match, it was easily accessible at local rivals, but luckily now good friends after all the bitterness of years ago, Boston Town. I fretted - should I go, or would it be better if I stayed away? Yes, I am a worrier, but I wanted to do the right thing; did not want to be in the way.

Both Chris Cook and Roy Hackford offered to pick me up, and Craig Singleton urged me to att end. In the end Maureen and I decided to go t ogether. Nobody knew my anxieties better than she did, and I welcomed her support. However I was still nervous, although meeting up with groundsman Nobby Croston and Sandra Richmond settled the nerves a little.

Then chairman David Newton came across to speak to us, followed by Neil Kempster, Mike Hardy, Craig Singleton, and Lewis and John Thorogood, and things became a little easier. Lewis and John asked us to go and sit with them, and it was funny having to ask the names of some of the United players. United were leading 2-0 at half-time, and I found having a cuppa in the directors room at the interval a little st range. Eventually we won 4-0, and I moved towards the dressing room area and chatted with a lot of people. They were all pleasant and obviously pleased to see us, and I began to wonder why I had been so apprehensive.

The chairman came over again and apologised because he would be unable to attend my forthcoming testimonial match because of a family wedding. He asked if, in fact, I was writing a book about my time at United, and if he would be featured in it. It would not be the last time he asked the question.

We left the Tattershall Road ground at about 10pm, relieved, and content at how the first meeting with everyone since my retirement had gone.

Nerves were again in overdrive when I woke up on Saturday July 9th -the day of my testimonial match, Boston United v Peterborough United. Elder statesmen among United fans could tell you of a few battles between these two teams in years gone by. It was raining heavily early in the morning, so heavily in fact that I began to wonder if the pitch would be playable, especially as the referee was Premier League official, Kevin Friend who had abandoned games on his previous two visits to York Street.

Luckily one of the assistant referees, Steve Ross, had passed the pitch as fit for play, and the rain had stopped before I met Kevin for a pre-match chat. We were able to joke about his past history at the Jakeman's Stadium. He had abandoned a league match against Nuneaton Town in the 44th minute because of a severe frost which was making the ground dangerous, and he had also called a halt to a pre-season friendly with Leeds United when a storm flooded the pitch. I am pleased he did not complete his hat-trick on this occasion.

There was a warm welcome from staff and supporters, but it was strange going to the ground without having any work to do. It was good to see former director, John Drewnicki, had come to support my testimonial, and players like Zak Mills, who had moved to Grimsby Town in the close season, and Derrick Nuttell and Darren Munton from a previous era. Another ex-Pilgrim David Farrell was involved with thePeterborough squad.

150

John and long time friend, Peterborough United's Director of Football, Barry Fry

The Posh had agreed to play at Boston thanks to my long-standing friend, Barry Fry, Director of Football at Peterborough, and one of the real characters of the game. Our friendship developed from the days when United and his Barnet were non-League rivals. The inimitable Barry took charge of proceedings, arranged photographs and ushered me to lead the teams onto the pitch. It was a proud moment as the fans gave me a great reception, and Maureen, and daughters Lisa and Katie, with their partners, David and Mark, were in the stand.

It was an entertaining match which, fittingly, ended in a 1-1 draw. Another good friend, Peter Jones, who had arranged for the game to be refereed by a Premier League official, was also present with his wife Jane.

The chairman, directors and Boston United Supporters Association had arranged a reception in the Pilgrim Lounge for staff, supporters, guests and friends, although the chairman was unable to attend because of a family wedding. It was a special, moving, but at the same time, relaxed evening, not only for me but also for two other dedicated servants of the club who had decided to retire, mainly for health reasons.

Jim Knight, who had played a major role in keeping the stadium ship-shape, and groundsman Keith (Nobby to pretty well everyone) Croston, who had worked wonders on the pitch, received much-deserved gifts.

David Newton's tribute was read by vice-chairman, Neil Kempster, and it was gratifying, if a little embarrassing, to receive his thanks for "an incredible 38 years of service to Boston United Football Club." He continued: "During those times you have seen some amazing ups, and some very significant downs, but you kept going throughout . "You have made many long lasting friendships, and you did your bit to help keep the club going through difficult times.

"The nine years since we took over in 2007 have just flown by, and I would like to thank you in particular for the work you carried out during that period. We have been on quite a journey together, and I am pleased to say that the club is in much better shape now, although there still remains a lot to do, not least promotion to the National League.

"The club has been transformed into a club at the heart of the community, where we use the Boston United brand to encourage as many people as possible to get active, and reap the benefits that sport and exercise can bring to everyone's lives. "We will continue to do our best to move the club forward and build on the firm roots that you have helped nurture over the years."

Chris Cook - described by the chairman as "another legend at this wonderful football club" - presented me with a very nice glass plaque and wrist watch . Craig Singleton interviewed me about my time with United, and the answers seemed to go down well. Some of the ex-players attending also got up and said some lovely words which was nice to hear.

It was a very enjoyable evening, an antidote to the retirement blues.

The Epilogue

My passion is for non-League football. I have an interest in the game at the highest level, drenched as it is in seemingly a non-stop supply of money, and forever surrounded by hype, but my big love is for the non -League game where I have rubbed shoulders with so many like-minded people. My admiration is for those who keep the game ticking over at a lower level and their supporters who often shun the star team to follow their local side.

The fact that I have been made President of Boston United enables me to continue to have a close-up of the club's activities, and performances home and away, and allows me to re-trace the trips around the country which I have made so often, re-acquainting myself with old friends and contacts and keeping up to date with new arrivals on what is an increasingly competitive part of the game.

My "bible" is the Non-League Paper. Its success over recent years highlights the big following for the non-League game throughout the country and I read every word from front page to the back.

Continuing to follow United up and down the country also allows me to run the rule over many players and I also attend, in addition, many matches lower down the pyramid. There is a much closer scrutiny of the non-League scene these days by the big clubs following the much-publicised rise of players like Leicester City's England international Jamie Vardy. I believe it could be the source of much more untapped talent and a viable alternative to the recruitment of so many foreign players at all levels of the elite game.

It is no easy option to play non-League football. The standard improves every year-you only have to look at all divisions of the Vanarama National League - and clubs are going full-time at levels lower than ever before. It is almost essential to have a team of full-time professionals to stand any chance of promotion to League Two.

Every year teams emerge from the shadows with new backing and big ambitions. It is not easy to attract top part-time players to a club like Boston United, and it is difficult to compete with wages being offered by some other teams. You can only hope that clubs are not being too reckless. We all know what happened to our own favourite club, and what a battle it has been - and still is - to fight the way back to the top echelons of the non-League game. My opinion is that survival, alone, has been a triumph given the circumstances that have surrounded the club.

Of course, in some cases where players work on good wages outside the game and also are on lucrative part-time soccer contracts, they would probably have to take a drop in income to join, say, one of the less well-off League Two clubs. That, perhaps, is one reason why the non-League game continues to improve.

But it can be hard, tiring work to be a part-time footballer, and also prove testing for a manager. Long journeys in midweek, particularly if they follow another long trip on the previous Saturday, can really sap the energy of players with a daytime job. Is training that week a good idea, or not? Probably not. But when does a manager get his ideas over to the players?

The use of statistics, and fitness sciences, have filtered down to non-League football, or followed managers around. Good or bad for part-time players? Or overkill? A subject for discussion among the enthusiasts.I am glad to hear the opinions, and be part of the discussions and, now aged 70, not too old, I hope, to take in new ideas.

During my short retirement I have also learned a little more about the "outside" world as a poll clerk at the county council and general elections, thanks to the suggestion of Boston United Supporters Association secretary Pauline Chapman who works for Boston Borough Council. Ironically, many people wanted to chat about United while casting their vote.

I have also worked as a stand-in delivery driver for Dave Henton's Boston Anorak Company when his regular driver Graham Barnett was recovering from an operation . I really enjoyed driving around the county, meeting customers and discovering businesses that were new to me.

Dave has been a good friend for many years, and a long-time devoted Boston United supporter, and was part of a reminder of an aspect of travelling in support of the team that makes you wonder why we still do it.

There have been many disappointments on the field, and despair on journeys to and from matches. The two things were combined on an early season trip to FC United of Manchester in 2017. We travelled in Dave's car, but he could not drive because his leg was in plaster, and he walked with the aid of crutches following a recent operation on his foot, so United Chief Executive, Mike Hardy, was at the wheel. The outward journey was fine. We parked up at the Broadhurst Park Stadium, enjoyed the hospitality of a three-course lunch, settled down to watch the match, and that was when the trouble started. United were two goals down in no time at all, and early in the second half had striker Greg Smith sent off. He was soon followed into the dressing room when Brad McGowan was given a red card.

Down to nine men, we managed to pull a goal back, but it was another defeat . Bad enough, but that was only the start of our troubles. Dave's car wouldn't start, and was only brought to life with the aid of jump leads masterminded by the home team's Chief Executive. We were on our way but, after only a few miles, the car would not accelerate. Thanks to the wonder of mobile 'phones we were able to contact Honda who advised us to try to reach a safe place and wait for assistance. Going onto the M62 and travelling towards Saddleworth Moor, the car really struggled to cope with the hills before we limped into Hartshead Moor Services, near Huddersfield . It was 6-SSpm, and we were advised that assistance was on its way. It arrived at 8-20pm, and the diagnosis did not improve our mood. The turbo had gone. The only way back to Boston was on a low -loader . The car was loaded and we had travelled only about 200 yards across the Services when the mechanic told us that he had been instructed to take the car off and we would have to wait for AA Recovery. It would, he said, be a wait of only about five minutes. That was at 8-S0pm. We sat on the lorry park and waited, and wait ed. The recovery vehicle arrived at 10-25pm . We re-started our journey back to Boston at 10-40pm, after struggling to get the stricken owner comfortable for the long ride.

After calling at Heckington to drop Mike Hardy at his home , we arrived at Dave's house at Haltoft End at 12-59am, one minute before the law said that the driver must have a rest. After a wait of 15 minutes, the car was unloaded, and I reached home at 1-45am!

It was all reminiscent of past travelling dramas such as when the coach caught fire in the middle of Huddersfield, when we had to borrow the home club's bus after a breakdown at Carlisle, and when we had a puncture on the way home from Oxford United. On reflection, that was a part of working for Boston United I did not enjoy. And it is no more pleasureable when you are President and su pport er.

It may come as a surprise to many, but the busiest time for a football club administrator can be in the summer. Not so in retirement, but, luckily for me, the Non-League Paper is still published and , with no games being played, has the space and time to reflect on the wider aspects of the game, particularly indulging in a spot of nostalgia .

Lo and behold, the first in a new series was headlined "Taunts, Insults and Bitterness with a Big Sense of Injust ic e." You've guessed it, yes, it was about the feud which developed between United and Dagenham and Redbridge in season 2001-02 when The Pilgrims squeezed past the Daggers to clinch promotion to League Two after a dramatic build-up to a tense final day of the season .

Mainly it was a war of words between the two managers, Steve Evans and Garry Hill, who insisted to the very end that United had cheated their way to success, which was re-lived in the arti cle.

The exchange of insults, no doubt , remains in the memories of both sets of fans. Some will have thought them demeaning, childish, outrageous; others will have found the situation exciting and funny. The article revealed that United legend,

155

goalkeeper Paul Bastock, thought it was "The funniest yearof my life."

Full-back Mark Clifford is quoted as expressing a different point of view. He thought the Evans' outbursts were deliberate and calculated. "Steve was fantastic at creating something out of nothing," he is reported as saying. "Wherever we went there was always an issue that would get our backs up. We would go to places thinking the fans were against us, the officials were against us, the pundits were against us. But it made us perform."

Five years later it was ironical that Dagenham replaced stricken United in the Football League , while United suffered a double relegation, being refused re-admission to the Conference. No doubt Dagenham supporters were thinking "Justice at last " . The whole issue, however, is part of non-League football and Boston United hist ory, and I had an uncomfortable ringside seat as it evolved.

That article revealed that apparently Steve Evans no longer wished to talk about his Boston days, except to say: "No one has apologised more than me. No one was punished more. I made a mistake. Would I make that same mistake again? I'd rather jump out of a plane without a parachute. I totally regret it. It was embarrassing to me and, much worse, to my family."

For me it brought back bittersweet memories. Without Steve Evans' input it is unlikely that I would have tasted life as a General Manager of a club playing at Football League level. Nor, I believe, would I have faced the anguish of an allegation that could have brought a criminal conviction, a threat removed only after the trauma of a lengthy court appearance and many sleepless nights .

That, of course, was the lowest point of my 38-year career with Boston United, but there was also the battle for survival after that. I believe that the fight is still ongoing to remove the stigma of that period in the club's history, and the struggle continues to regain what many people believe is our rightful place in the Vanarama National League. I hope that I am still club President when it happens. At the moment, however, that dream seems a long way off .

As I write this, the battle is on to prevent a slip even further down the football pyramid as United are in the relegation zone in the National League North, manager Adam Murray having resigned and been replaced by Barnsley -based Craig Elliott who will be hoping to repeat the success he enjoyed with Shaw Lane .

While the 2017-18 season started in disappointing fashion for The Pilgrims, I have still enjoyed following them, especially as surprises have welcomed me at some of the clubs I have visited.

Take, for instance, the match date of October 7th 2017 when we visited AFC Telford

United. Waiting to greet me, after many years without contact, was Mike Ferriday, secretary of the former Telford United club. He introduced me to some of the sponsors who were enjoying a pre-match meal in their executive box. On the wall of the Smith Room - named after their former chairman who was on the Conference Management Committee with me - was a framed shirt signed by Everton players when Telford visited Goodison Park in the FA Cup back in 1988.

In the previous round, Telford had been drawn away to Lincoln City, and Telford manager Stan Storton, unable to watch the Imps himself, had asked me to "spy" on them in a match before the cup tie. In this game, Lincoln won a penalty and my report to Stan included details of where the penalty taker placed his spot kick. Lo and behold, in the cup tie between Telford and Lincoln, the City won a late penalty which the Telford goalkeeper, Kevin Charlton, saved by following my advice, and Telford went on to win to earn the money-spinning tie away to Everton. Mike flattered me somewhat by telling his pals that it was me who helped Telford make a lot of money that day.

Those present showed great interest in Boston United and their ground development plans, and also knew a lot about the town itself, particularly about the issue of immigration. For 20 minutes or so, it was like giving an after-dinner speech, but it was a gesture that I very much appreciated and a reminder that football camaraderie is not only about what happens on the field of play.

I was caught up in another surprise on Wednesday November 8th 2017 when, in my capacity as a scout for Swansea City, I visited Sleaford Town's well-appointed ground. They were playing Wisbech Town in a United Counties Premier League fixture which had attracted Yorkshire Television cameras because it was a big night for a Boston United legend. Paul Bastock, at the age of 47, was poised to equal the record number of appearances by a goalkeeper in professional football.

That record, which many predicted would never be broken, stood at 1249 appearances, and Paul equalled it by playing in that game, attracting a lot of national publicity in the process. He has, of course, since passed the record and, all being well, will have put more space between himself and previous holder, England international and world-class goalkeeper, Peter Shilton, by the time you read this.

I was grabbed by the TV crew at Sleaford to say a few words about Paul, a great advert for non-League football, and was happy to do so. The film went out on the Calendar news programme.

I remember well the day Paul signed for Boston United. It was at the start of the 1992-93 season when Peter Morris was manager, and Ernie Moss was his assistant.

United were playing a series of pre-season games against local sides and a new goalkeeper was scheduled to play in a game away to Spilsby Town in the Grace Swan Cup.

Paul Bastock
Boston United record appearance holder

That man was Paul Bastock , but, held up by heavy traffic and not knowing the area, he was late and, despite my wife Maureen and Glen Maddison, waiting to take him to Spilsby, he did not play in the game which, incidentally, was won by what I believe is a United record of 12-0. He did, however, agree terms and sign after the game , and went on to become a big favourite with supporters, a club legend, in fact, who set a club appearance record with more than 670 games.

The Redditch-born goalkeeper, who played for Coventry City when they won the FA Youth Cup in 1987, and played his first Football League game for Cambridge United, went on to settle in Boston, marry chairman Pat Malkinson's daughter, Ann, and is now a popular figure around the district where he runs a window-cleaning business. He has played for something like 17 clubs to reach his record.

He is very much part of Boston United's history and, now, one of the game's record holders, a man it is a privilege to know and to have worked alongside. Paul's amazing story is an example of how far the tentacles emanating from Boston United have reached. There are so many people who have been involved with the club, people who live all over the country, indeed beyond, like ex-player Graham Potter, who has hit the headlines by his success as a manager in Sweden.

It has, indeed, given me great satisfaction to have known so many of them, and to have been greeted by them on my travels.

All because I worked for Boston United for 38 years.

Thank you....

Over all my years in football I have made many friends, and received support and encouragement from lots and lots of people. To all of you I say a heartfelt thank you.

Most of all, however, I wish to pay tribute to my wife Maureen, and daughters Lisa and Katie for their never-ending t oler a n ce , support and under st a n ding. They have been brilliant.

This particular project, having the audacity of putting my story into print, owes much to the cajoling and encouragement, of George Wheatman, the support of Stuart Cropley, of Cropleys Suzuki - a long-standing friend and ally - and, in the final push, the skill of United legend, Chris Cook, not on the field of play this time but through his expertise in the world of design, printing and publishing.

My sincere thanks also go to Paul Cooper, of Ringrose Law, for his much appreciated advice, and to Ken Fox for giving me permission to tap into the invaluable United statistics that he has turned into such a useful website.

My rock, my wife, Maureen with daughters Katie (left) & Lisa (right)

Newspapers, Boston Standard, Boston Target and Lincolnshire Echo, kindly have given permission for me to use photographs which I believe have enhanced my efforts to review the many things that have happened in my years with Boston United.

Being presented with one of my many cars from Stewart Cropley of Cropleys Suzuki

Fantastic squad from the 70's celebrating another trophy win!

Right: Myself, Jim Kabia, Emlyn Hughes and Steve Thompson at Emlyn's Testimonial

An emotional moment celebrated in the Boardroom with players, staff & directors

Printed in Great Britain
by Amazon

79355742R00092